SUPERPOWERED

THE SECRET THAT HELPS EVERY ENTREPRENEUR ELIMINATE THE SUCK, 10X THEIR IMPACT, AND HAVE MORE FUN IN WORK AND LIFE

SUPERPOWERED

THE SECRET THAT HELPS EVERY ENTREPRENEUR ELIMINATE THE SUCK, 10X THEIR IMPACT, AND HAVE MORE FUN IN WORK AND LIFE

SHANNON WALLER | RYAN CASSIN | STEVEN NEUNER

ethos
collective

Printed in the United States of America

Published by Igniting Souls
PO Box 43, Powell, OH 43065
IgnitingSouls.com

LCCN: 2024912309
Paperback ISBN: 978-1-63680-325-8
Hardcover ISBN: 978-1-63680-326-5
e-book ISBN: 978-1-63680-327-2

Available in paperback, hardcover, e-book, and audiobook.

Any Internet addresses (websites, blogs, etc.) and telephone numbers printed in this book are offered as a resource. They are not intended in any way to be or imply an endorsement by Igniting Souls, nor does Igniting Souls vouch for the content of these sites and numbers for the life of this book.

Some names and identifying details may have been changed to protect the privacy of individuals.

The superscript symbol IP listed throughout this book is known as the unique certification mark created and owned by Instant IP™. Its use signifies that the corresponding expression (words, phrases, chart, graph, etc.) has been protected by Instant IP™ via smart contract. Instant IP™ is designed with the patented smart contract solution (US Patent: 11,928,748), which creates an immutable time-stamped first layer and fast layer identifying the moment in time an idea is filed on the blockchain. This solution can be used in defending intellectual property protection. Infringing upon the respective intellectual property, i.e. IP, is subject to and punishable in a court of law.

Table of Contents

Part Two: Supershift

Part Three: Superpowered

Foreword by Dan Sullivan

In our decades of entrepreneurial coaching, we've helped thousands of entrepreneurs discover their Unique Ability®— what they love and do best—because at Strategic Coach®, we know that when people live according to their purpose and passion, both their work life and personal life improve exponentially. I watched this play out for Shannon as she used her Unique Ability to develop The Strategic Assistant® Program and then The Strategic Coach® Team Programs to provide team members with the tools they need to grow and thrive on an entrepreneurial team. And she dramatically leveraged her capabilities and productivity when she added Nicole and then Katrina to her team as Support Partners.

Steven and Ryan's personal and business lives also offer proof of how adding the right "Whos" allows you to enjoy your business more and frees you up to spend quality time with the other important people in your life. They're passionate about the difference that having an entrepreneurial Executive Assistant makes in entrepreneurs' lives, and they help them work successfully with their EAs, equipping them with tools and strategies so that the EA is constantly growing, evolving, and providing higher levels of support.

Shannon, Steven, and Ryan show tremendous enthusiasm for helping other business leaders find the freedom and growth they've experienced for themselves, and Superpowered continues the theme of growth through leveraging others' talents that Ben Hardy and I presented in our books *Who Not How* and *10x Is Easier Than 2x.* I've seen firsthand how the principles of Superpowered have impacted members of Strategic Coach, and I look forward to seeing even more entrepreneurs discover the freedom that comes from leveraging their capabilities.

—Dan Sullivan, co-founder of Strategic Coach®, the World's Foremost Entrepreneur Coach and bestselling author of more than 30 books

Note to the Reader

Who knew a series of six podcasts would lead to a book? But here we are. When we closed the door on that last recording, we knew the message needed to go further. Too many entrepreneurs needlessly struggle.

So few understand the role of the Executive Assistant. It is quite possibly the most difficult role to fill. Yet, when done well, everyone we talk to agrees: it definitely sits on the top ten list of most important. And while, for the sake of brevity and clarity, we will refer to EAs with feminine pronouns, don't think this role is limited to women. Though 95% of our applicants fall in that category, we've hired men who've made outstanding Executive Assistants.

Honestly, we don't know what we'd do without our EAs. In fact, they're so important, you'll want to make certain you read to the end and hear their take on the relationship.

Perhaps you have a great Executive Assistant. If so, we invite you to read this through the lens that the slightest tweaks take you to the highest peaks. Look for tips on making your relationship with your EA even more Superpowered.

On the other hand, you might know you will never have an EA. In that case, this book will bring you a parable on purpose and leadership. Look for yourself in the pages and watch for concrete ways to become a better leader, communicator, teammate, delegator, and more. You'll discover that the principles that allow you to be a great leader in an entrepreneur-assistant relationship will also make you a great leader in other roles.

And if you've considered hiring an Executive Assistant but have all kinds of barriers keeping you from enjoying the freedom and growth this role can add, we hope this book allows you to get rid of the suck, 10x your impact, and have more fun in work and life.

PART ONE

Superstressed

A Tale of Two Entrepreneurs

Victor and Larry grew up down the street from one another. Friends from a young age, the two attended the same high school and college, and their fathers worked together at the local factory.

After graduation, Victor married and moved to his wife's hometown, a moderately sized place with a population of about 30,000. After working in the restaurant business for five years, he took his love of specialty coffees to the next level and opened his own corner coffee shop. His unique blends attracted patrons from every sector of town, and within two years, the overflow-only seating prompted him to open another location across town. Six years and three locations later, the young entrepreneur had built a small chain.

Larry had a similar story. He loved creating decadent desserts in the high-profile kitchens that gave him a start. But in the end, he knew these establishments squashed his creativity. In a town about thirty miles from his friend, Larry's one-of-a-kind specialty scones and croissants became an overnight success. Even the additional outdoor seating didn't accommodate his guests. Larry opened five bakeries in his town as well.

Finding vendors and staff, keeping manageable inventories, bookkeeping, and marketing consumed both men. Even with competent managers to handle scheduling and customer service, each man slept less than five hours a day, and date nights with their wives were unheard of. They started early each morning and filled at least two shifts at each location every week.

Even on those occasions when they took a shift off, the texts and phone calls never stopped, and both guys found themselves distracted thinking about the next day's agenda.

After graduation, the friends stayed in touch, and after starting their businesses, they met at one of their locations to enjoy a cup of coffee together at least once a month. It gave them time to catch up and vent. Their conversations nearly always included hopes of starting families, wondering how they'd have time to be great dads, staffing issues, and regretting the lack of availability to be creative in the kitchen anymore. As their endeavors grew, Larry had a difficult time making the monthly get-togethers, so they moved their coffee hours to once a quarter. Just after each entrepreneur opened his fifth location, the discussion took a turn.

Superstressed

"Sorry I'm late, Victor. I got held up in a meeting," Larry said as he motioned for one of his servers to bring his latte.

"No problem, friend. I'm just glad you could make it. I have big news."

"Me, too. That's what the meeting was about," Larry said just as his latte arrived.

"Okay, then. You first."

"I think I found a buyer for two of my shops." Larry sounded excited, but his facial expressions didn't match his tone.

Victor grew silent. Not sure what to say, he took a nice long drink of his coffee first. "But you just opened that new location."

"I know. But this opportunity came along, and I couldn't pass it up." Larry didn't sound convincing. "What's your news?" Victor thought his tone was a bit half-hearted. Still, he couldn't keep from beaming.

"Nicole and I are expecting a little girl in four months!"

"What!? You waited this long to tell me."

"We found out she was pregnant right after the last time you and I met, and I wanted to tell you in person. Besides that, you haven't really been answering many texts or phone calls recently."

Larry looked defeated. "How do you even have time to text me, Victor? This fifth store is killing me. Even with tremendous managers, I can't keep up. Madison's talking about leaving."

"I'm really sorry, man. It's been almost a year since Paul talked to us about hiring assistants. What happened?"

"I tried. I hired my wife's cousin to help with the books, but that didn't work out. Then, a friend was looking for work, so I paid him to manage inventories, but he'd never done anything like that before. Five locations was too much for him. I'm a little gun-shy when it comes to bringing on someone new right now. I'm hoping if I sell two stores, I can keep up again. Maybe I can spend more time with Madison and go back to creating fresh ideas for the menu every now and then."

Larry had resigned himself to never being able to grow his business, and he had scar tissue from so many disappointments in hiring. He knew he wouldn't be able to keep up the pace for long, but he believed he'd done everything he could. His wife, Madison, was tired of going to family parties alone and had told him if she had to live alone, she'd rather do it by herself. Larry felt as though he was losing his relationships, his business, and his passion.

Superpowered

Victor felt his friend's pain. After playing the game for five years, he knew the stress of keeping up with a growing business. However, he and Nicole had taken time to weigh their options before adding the fifth shop. At that time, he spent about seventy hours a week working in the shops and driving between them. Plus, he added another ten or more at home, keeping the books up to date and talking to suppliers. Like Larry, Victor considered selling. In fact, he'd gone one step further and entertained getting out completely, but his wife reminded him how much he loved owning the business, exploring new coffee flavors, and adding new sweets to the menu.

As he struggled with his future, Victor contacted Paul. This friend of the men's fathers was a more seasoned entrepreneur, and he shared his experience with both Victor and Larry. He recommended they hire Executive Assistants, explaining the advantages of an assistant as well as the process he used to find the young man who currently allowed him to focus on the parts of the business he was best suited for.

Paul described a person who fielded his emails, managed his calendar, and knew everything going on in his personal life, so his work schedule never interfered with his family schedule. Having the assistant allowed Paul to take his family on lengthy, uninterrupted vacations because their communication styles and cadences were so similar. The assistant understood the entrepreneur's goal and made decisions that reflected those goals. Before he left the coffee shop that day, Paul emphasized again the need to hire the right person.

When Victor talked to Nicole about hiring an assistant later that evening, she immediately volunteered to quit her job and take on some of his responsibilities. "If I do it, we can save the money you would pay an assistant," she said.

"You know you'll hate it," Victor told her. "You love doing interior design. And would we save enough to make up for what you'd lose?" Victor did not want his wife to give up her passion so he could live his. He had also taken to heart Paul's emphasis on finding someone he could trust who also had the passion and personality to take ownership of the position. His wife's heart just wouldn't be in it.

Why Did You Become an Entrepreneur?

While Victor moved forward, Larry stayed stuck on the Freedom/Growth seesaw. With just one corner coffee shop, Larry felt free to create in the kitchen and enjoy his entrepreneurship. However, with each step of growth, the pastry chef lost a bit of his freedom. Each grand opening brought a slight shift to the seesaw.

When Victor and Nicole started discussing whether to sell or find an assistant and open their fifth location, Nicole asked Victor a key question: "Why did you open that first coffee shop, Victor?"

The question stopped him in his tracks. He hadn't thought about his purpose in owning a coffee place in years. "Well," he laughed, "it definitely wasn't so I could run myself ragged and feel like I was losing my mind."

He realized every reason he had to open the very first shop still existed. "I wanted to create new flavors, be my own boss, and live life on my own terms. Plus, providing for the family so you could be the stay-at-home mom you'd always dreamed of is important. But, looking at my schedule now, I know I want the freedom to choose what I do. I want to be a part of this family we're talking about. I don't want to be an extra person at the dinner table once a week. I want our kids to know me and eventually be a part of the business if they choose to."

The thirty-something couple knew in order for Victor to fulfill his purpose, take back his time, build their relationship, create the income their family needed, and sustain his health something had to change—and it needed to be immediate and intentional.

Victor employed a service to help him find the right assistant. This young lady took control of Victor's schedule, giving him time to cook for his wife and experiment with pastry recipes so he could offer new specials on his menus each month. Additionally, Victor had always loved working the counter at the shops, interacting with the team and the customers, and sharing his secrets with his staff. With an assistant taking care of the day-to-day, this coffee shop entrepreneur began spending one day a week in each coffee shop and left his weekends free to spend with his wife. Plus, having an assistant on the payroll opened the door for Victor and Nicole to start the baby conversation.

Missed Opportunities

Unfortunately, too many entrepreneurs look more like Larry than Victor. Our greatest strengths become our biggest weaknesses. Since we can do almost anything at least adequately, we do almost everything—usually less than adequately. As self-starters who are ultra-competent and competitive, we forge ahead, conquering what others don't do to our standards and micromanaging everything we allow another to touch.

Most can keep up the pace for at least six months to a year, and often, entrepreneurial endeavors require that kind of sacrifice for a time. Entrepreneurs thrive on striving toward results and success. However, after the first growth spurt, the "do it myself" philosophy begins to rob the entrepreneur like a thief in the night. While they think their only forfeitures are sleep, fun times, and relationships, these innovators become so embedded in the quagmire of day-to-day details that they can't see the big picture anymore. What started out as a way to reach new levels of freedom and growth has become an endless uphill treadmill.

The hours and hours of hard work take their toll on the entrepreneur's health as well as personal and professional relationships. And it doesn't take long for the stress to turn a calendar into a double-booked nightmare. Between the business messages and spam, important emails get missed. Like Victor and Larry, date nights are like mirages in the desert, and the business owner's to-do list begins to feel like a wish list.

Worse still, business opportunities get missed. Mundane tasks become like weeds in a garden, choking out entrepreneurs' creativity and blinding them to lucrative endeavors. They don't have time to add anything to the business model because they can't keep up with their current calendars and task lists. And on a personal level, a business birthed out of passion and excitement becomes a chore. What should bring joy and add fun to entrepreneurs' lives turns into an anchor weighing them down and pulling them under.

The Superpowered Scale

Most entrepreneurs fall somewhere between Victor and Larry on the Superpowered Scale[IP]. Victor hit Transformation level when he allowed his mindset to move to Superpowered, and the result transformed his coffee shops as well as his personal life. Because he unlocked the secret, he and his wife started dating again. He had time to golf as well as explore new coffee and latte flavors. The increased revenue allowed him to upgrade his wireless connection, and his coffee shops became meeting places for remote business owners.

On the other end of the spectrum, Larry flailed. He remained Superstressed, afraid to take the next step, and resigned to working countless hours for minimal returns until he retires or someone comes along and steals the business out from under him because he is too tired to care if they offer him below market value for his shops.

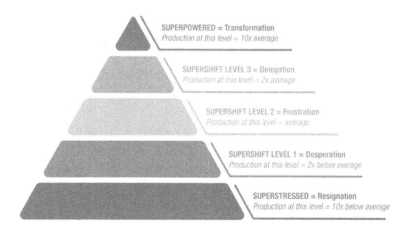

SUPERPOWERED = Transformation
Production at this level = 10x average

SUPERSHIFT LEVEL 3 = Delegation
Production at this level = 2x average

SUPERSHIFT LEVEL 2 = Frustration
Production at this level = average

SUPERSHIFT LEVEL 1 = Desperation
Production at this level = 2x below average

SUPERSTRESSED = Resignation
Production at this level = 10x below average

Resignation-The Superstressed Level of the Scale

Larry had moved to the level of resignation—a place with no hope. Creativity ceases, and the entrepreneur can't remember why he or she wanted to start the business in the first place. These entrepreneurs stop looking for fun from any part of life. Simply existing becomes the norm, and they expect nothing more. Many start to ask, "What's wrong with me?" Productivity crashes to below average, and it feels as if throwing in the towel is the only thing left to do.

Between Victor and Larry's approaches, we find a group of entrepreneurs in Supershift mode. Entrepreneurs move between these three levels as they shift their mindset from Resignation to Transformation—from Superstressed to Superpowered.

Desperation-The Lowest Supershift Level

One step before Resignation, we find Desperation. On the verge of burnout, these entrepreneurs long for a way out, and when they don't find it, they move into Resignation. Larry went through this stage when he tried to sell two of his shops. Victor even lived here for a thought or two; however, a shift in mindset sent him up the Scale while his friend spiraled downward in an over-caffeinated mess.

If people stay in the Desperation or Resignation zones for too long, they begin to sabotage relationships. They look for distractions to avoid the pain, and these distractions often become addictions. Marriages suffer, friendships get forgotten, and children feel abandoned.

Frustration-The Second Supershift Level

Many entrepreneurs enter a striving mode at the center of the Scale—the Supershift Level of Frustration. Starting a business is hard work, and for a time, it might not seem like much fun. When we strive for too long and don't see results, we feel the pull of Frustration. Our production hits maintenance level, and let's face it, average isn't really the modus operandi for the true entrepreneur.

Some business owners recognize this stage as merely growing pains. They push forward because they remember why they started the business. Others plummet, and if it's not the first time they've been in this level of frustration, they may fall very hard.

Unfortunately, these levels are not cumulative. They don't automatically build on one another or stop you on your way down. Those who don't continue to progress forward eventually fall, skipping by any Supershift levels they've conquered right back into Resignation. This doesn't mean you won't have days or weeks of frustration or feel desperation when pressure builds; however, consistently living below your full potential will ultimately pull you back to the bottom of the scale.

Delegation-The Top Supershift Level

Entrepreneurs who use Frustration to their advantage rise to the level of Delegation. They understand the next Supershift point—you cannot grow alone. Entrepreneurs at the Delegation stage begin to bring on team members. The extra help temporarily alleviates some of the pain, but without the intention you find in the Superpowered zone, it becomes like trying to heal a broken arm with a splint.

Delegation allows you to double your efforts, and life starts looking not so bad. You can think more tactically because you have a team to get the job done. But if you're doing it right, you'll sense there's more.

Transformation-Superpowered

And that "more" is what this book is about. Each of us and thousands of entrepreneurs we've worked with have moved into the "more." We've discovered how to achieve our dreams, realize our visions, and help grow the people around us. The tension between Growth and Freedom disappears. The two areas of success no longer compete for the top spot. To move into this space, make a list of your dreams. Take a moment and finish these statements. How do you respond when you're over your head in tasks that should be easy but bog you down?

- I wish I had time to . . .

- I dream of the day when I can just . . .

In the Superpowered zone, these thoughts become obsolete because your EA creates time and embraces the tasks that keep you from fulfilling your dreams. We've already hinted at the Secret that will help you Eliminate the Suck,

10x your impact, and allow you to have more fun in your work and life. But keep reading because we've just scratched the surface. When you reach this place of Transformation, you'll be grateful you embraced the secret to being Superpowered.

> I had to develop a new way of being, a new identity that matched what I believed I was called to achieve. —Steven Neuner

Do you feel more like Larry or Victor in your entrepreneurial life?
Or maybe you fall somewhere in between.
Would you like to know where you are right now on the Scale?
Take a moment to visit SuperpoweredBook.com
and answer ten simple questions to get your
Superpowered Scorecard.

Takeaways

1. Attempting to do everything on your own on a long-term basis means you do everything less adequately.
2. Don't allow your biggest strengths to become your biggest weaknesses. Stop micromanaging!
3. Shift your mindset from Resignation to Transformation—from Superstressed to Superpowered.
4. To progress up the Superpowered Scale, change needs to be immediate and intentional.
5. Dissolve the tension between Growth and Freedom by hiring an EA who creates time and embraces the tasks that keep you from fulfilling your dreams.

Riding the Seesaw

The problem is never the problem.
The problem is not knowing how to think about the problem.

—Dan Sullivan, Co-Founder of Strategic Coach®

Steven's Backstory

I started my entrepreneurial endeavors in insurance. My wife "temporarily" left her teaching job to help me get the business off the ground and out of our guest bedroom. I focused on growing the business, and she took care of every other role in the company. I'm not sure I can ever tell her how grateful I am for her help. However, we both freely admit—it was awful! Even though the business was growing, we were miserable.

If you feel like you're on the entrepreneurial seesaw, we have compassion for you. That was our story until a friend introduced me to Strategic Coach.

Ryan and Steven started Superpowers to help entrepreneurs find freedom and growth. They each mentored several individuals to help them get off the seesaw, and both men were so excited about their discoveries that they freely shared. They wanted everyone to enjoy their business instead of living in drudgery.

Meet Ryan

Believe it or not, I started out in politics. My best friend from college and I did political consulting for almost ten years before we sold our business. I had less than zero idea of how to get a business off the ground when we got our first check from a client. We moved quickly from not knowing how to start an LLC to growing a business someone else wanted to buy.

The Entrepreneurs' Organization (EO) Accelerator program helped us move up quickly. I hate to admit it, but I never would have opened that door if a client hadn't threatened to fire us if I didn't join the program. I dreamed of joining the big kids at the over one-million-dollar-a-year point, but when I started with EO Accelerator, that seemed impossible. Fortunately, our vast transformation and the training from Strategic Coach taught me how to hire the right staff, create processes, deliver predictable service, and sell consistently.

Entrepreneurs want to be free to spend their time and money in a way that promotes what matters most to them and those they love, free to enjoy their health and relationships, and free to fulfill their purpose. Walking hand in hand with that passion for freedom, we find the entrepreneur's deep desire to create something bigger than themselves. These pioneers won't settle for sufficient and static.

Too many times, though, instead of freedom and growth moving together smoothly like horses on the merry-go-round, they end up on opposite ends of the seesaw. Without all the pieces in place, when the new business owner works in and expands his Unique Ability®, he stifles growth. To compensate, entrepreneurs begin to focus on growing the business rather than living their passions. They learn marketing and add to their teams. In the process, they lose themselves in the busyness of the business. Every time the focus shifts to raising one side of the seesaw, the other suffers. We believe the Executive Assistant is the key to jumping off the Freedom vs. Growth seesaw and grabbing the reins of true success.

Nearly every kid has been caught on one side of a seesaw. Either the person on the other end is too light and can't bring us back up, or our friend purposely moves all his weight to the back of the fulcrum, letting us hang in the air indefinitely.

The same thing happens to entrepreneurs. We get trapped on this endless up-and-down ride, working in freedom for a time and then moving into growth mode because revenue drops or a business opportunity we can't pass up. Sadly, all we really want is for our freedom and growth to coexist peacefully. And this freedom/growth seesaw keeps us stuck on the most difficult three levels of the Scale. The Frustration of being caught on one side or the other leads to Desperation and Resignation. And if we don't completely give up, the up and down goes on and on relentlessly. We want you to know it's time to jump off and move with confidence and inspiration, avoiding the hard bump on the other end.

Backstage

From high school musicals to Broadway productions, every stage has one thing in common: a host of backstage performers. Costumes, props, grips, sound, lighting, flymen, and more produce the magic you don't see from the theater seats. Still, the production wouldn't be the same without them. Disney understands the importance of the unseen players. Their theme parks don't have employees. Even those who stock shelves in the stores, paint the lovely ornaments, decorate the castle at night, set off the fireworks shows, and retrieve the garbage are seen as vital components of the play and take on the title of cast member.

A great director recognizes that the back of the house is just as important as the faces on the promo posters. Even a high school drama teacher would never attempt to fulfill the multitude of roles needed to pull off a tremendous performance.

Much like a theater, your business has a stage and a backstage. The stage is any place where you and your team interact with clients and patrons. As the owner, you are one of the primary actors. Your customers feel more valued when they see and talk to you. Coffee shop regulars develop greater loyalty when they get to know the entrepreneur in charge. And even if you're the creative who prefers to let someone else be the face of the company, every time you allow the backstage tedium to distract you from your passion, you climb back on the seesaw and slip down the Scale.

The backstage of your company will look much like the backstage at the theater. When people peek behind the curtain, they'll see the clutter. Emails and invoices pile up. Your calendar looks like the disarray of wardrobe between acts on the stage. Questions come from every side. Most inquiries have little to do with stage direction, but someone has to answer.

The Executive Assistant is the entrepreneur's Stage Manager. These vital players make certain the curtain rises just as the first note of the orchestra plays. They organize every pile and pass to you only what is necessary to make the production a success. As the director, you no longer worry about whether the spotlight moves correctly or messages get delivered to the appropriate members of the cast because the Stage Manager—the Executive Assistant—takes care of every unseen, yet essential, moving part.

Confusion and Self-Limiting Beliefs

You have plenty of vision for your dreams, ambitions, and aspirations. But the seesaw gets in the way. It assaults this hidden relationship that holds the key to bringing you up out of the mire. Consider the immense list of things you keep track of every day that weigh you down. Follow-ups, project micro-management, calendar details, to-do lists, and more disrupt your creativity. You start strong, but then your brain interrupts when it wonders if your accountant got the paperwork she needed.

Despite the value, entrepreneurs have a variety of reasons for avoiding an assistant. Larry, from our story at the beginning, clearly demonstrated one of the top arguments for putting off hiring an Executive Assistant. Some small business owners begin expanding by hiring family members or friends who lack the specific talents needed to fill the position. After a few misfires, the entrepreneur becomes gun shy;

he or she develops scar tissue from all the pain, and if they've been injured by personal relationships as well, the wound runs deeper. Later, we'll go into greater detail on finding the right Who for the job. However, for right now, let's just say we can't overstate the importance of finding someone with the right skills and an entrepreneurial mindset who understands your communication style so they can help close loops in your brain.

Another holdback is the time and stress factor. These entrepreneurs constantly worry about unanswered emails and missing appointments. Perhaps you or someone you know has fallen into the trap of "I don't have time to hire someone right now." Every aspect of the business seems to be spinning out of control—you feel like you're losing your mind. Adding one more cog to the wheel appears to cause more stress, and the time required to interview and train seems too valuable to give up. However, we forget that little lesson from science class—every time we add a wheel to the pulley, the load is easier to move.

Unfortunately, all this stress and confusion increases your self-limiting beliefs. Nearly everyone starts with a few self-limiting beliefs.

- **Imposter Syndrome:** I'm too young (or too old). I don't have enough education or experience. I'm not good enough.
- **Fear of Failure:** If I take risks and fail, it might ruin my business and my reputation.
- **Perfectionism and Inability to Delegate:** Can someone really do this faster than me? I can't move forward until I get this right. I can't launch until everything is flawless. Should I expect someone else to do the things I don't want to do?

- **Scarcity Mindset:** I don't have time. I don't have enough money. I don't have enough customers.
- **Fear of Rejection:** If I put myself or my ideas out there, someone may reject or criticize me.
- **Comparison to Others:** I don't measure up.
- **Resistant to Change:** I prefer to keep things as they are, even if they aren't working.
- **Lack of Confidence:** I doubt my abilities and decisions. I'm not sure I have what it takes to succeed.
- **Fixed Mindset:** I can't improve, so there's no point in trying to grow or learn.
- **Comfort Zone:** It's easier to keep doing things myself than to train someone else—especially if I have to do it a number of times. It's safer to stick with what I know.

And that's not an exhaustive list. We create these perceptions throughout our lifetime to rationalize pain and protect ourselves from future hurt. But left to themselves, they become weights around our necks unless we dismiss and overcome them—and that's not easy to do. And if we're riding the seesaw, we begin to believe the lies that the busyness of trying to do it all creates. We write new self-limiting beliefs or confirm those we've been carrying around.

- See, I told you I didn't have what it takes.
- I knew I wouldn't be good at this.
- I suck at being an entrepreneur.
- I'm taking time away from my family and friends— I'm not really a good person.

Which of those self-limiting beliefs resonate with you?
or What other statements hold you back?

These lies compound as we're forced to work harder outside our Unique Ability, and the result can become debilitating. We have to counteract these statements by recognizing them as false, remembering and celebrating our past achievements, and changing our mindset around them.

Allow us to share Eric's story of the power of a changed mindset:

I met Shannon at my first Strategic Coach workshop, and I shared with her the struggle I had finding people to work for me. I knew I wanted to grow into my 10x future self, and I had begun to realize it wasn't about me doing more, working harder, working faster. I knew that would never work. It might take me to a 2x, but even that would be hard.

I didn't have the concept of Dan's book Who Not How® *yet, and I was telling Shannon about my frustrations with the people I was working with. I described my situation for about twenty minutes, and Shannon came back with just one comment.*

She told me, "Well, you need people on your team who are like you."

I said, "OK, that's great, but what is that?"

Shannon replied, "They have to be wicked smart," and walked away.

She might as well have smacked me in the face. I struggled through middle school and high school. On that day, Eric Rothman was still in fifth grade, feeling anything but wicked smart. Suddenly, Shannon forced me to enter a painful thought process—a process that convinced me who I really am is so different from who I thought I was.

In that room, Shannon created the distinction. That was a shattering moment—as if the glass ceiling above my head came crashing down. Eric Rothman is wicked smart. And after I started to believe it, I said to myself, "Wow! If that's true, I can no longer ever have people around me who aren't uniquely talented in what they do and wicked smart."

I got it—no more hiring tacticians. If I wanted to grow, I had to hire wicked smart people uniquely talented in their domain for the purpose of freeing me up 500 hours a year.

So, there I was with this new distinction—I was wicked smart with the new understanding that each person I hire has the potential to give me 500 hours a year. I started thinking, "How many of these people do I want?" Each person became a point of leverage.

And that's when the transformation started.

I've come to realize the mindset of "grow a little and then grow a little more" doesn't work. You can never produce a 10X outcome with that thinking. —Eric Rothman

In particular, we—Shannon, Ryan, and Steven—want to focus on the limiting beliefs that keep you from adding to your staff. Many are like Eric—they can't see how great they are. Eric was missing a key component. He needed a mindset shift regarding who he really was. Others don't think they deserve an Executive Assistant. You may have thought to yourself:

- I haven't accomplished enough yet.
- I don't have the business organized enough to hand it over to someone else.
- I should be able to do it all myself.
- I'm not sure there's enough work to justify hiring someone to support me alone.
- I don't know if I can afford it or justify the added expense.
- Other hires are more important—my team needs more help than I do.

Some in this camp will hire assistants for others in their organization while they keep trudging through the muck with their waders on. For some reason, his employees bring enough value to the company to merit some help, but the entrepreneur continues to go it alone.

Steven's Self-Limiting Beliefs

It wasn't until AFTER my team convinced me to hire my first Executive Assistant that I had time to figure out why I dug my heels in so deeply at the thought. Some deep work digging into my past revealed that I didn't believe I was good enough or deserved to spend so much on myself personally. My subconscious had trapped me in a hole of mediocrity. I could only pursue good—not great—for my life. I lived like I was ready for the big game. I was an All-Star in the minors. No one in my circle would have guessed I was afraid to leave the minor leagues. Somewhere deep inside I had convinced myself if I tried to go big, I would self-destruct. At the same time, I knew I was under-indexing my potential. Positive I would blow the biggest opportunities, I avoided trying for them. I believed I wasn't cut out for the main stage.

"I can't afford to hire an Executive Assistant" becomes a big obstacle to many business owners. We would argue, "You can't afford NOT to hire an Executive Assistant." With the right Who in place, you can 10x your own production as you focus on honing your craft and focusing on your purpose. And as we go through the next chapters, we'll demonstrate how the right talented individual can increase productivity across your company.

Don't Set Yourself Up for Failure

Perhaps you had the ideal setup when you started your business. You had the right training and developed a tremendous five-year plan. The internships you chose prepared you well—or so you thought. Growing pains are a real thing in business, and they can bring on self-doubt and feed our limiting beliefs. The reality is we need more than a vision and a carefully thought-out business strategy. To truly succeed, we need some key relationships, and the most important of these may be the Executive Assistant.

Too many resist the idea of being supported, especially those who want to make certain the rest of their team has adequate support. At Strategic Coach, the premier coaching program and community for successful entrepreneurs, co-founder Dan Sullivan stresses the vital role of a Strategic Assistant®.

Steven's Struggle With Hiring His EA

Usually, when a leader at Strategic Coach tells us to do something, I do it. But I just couldn't jump on this. I delayed getting myself an assistant to the point my team finally staged an intervention.

"Steven, we appreciate the way you love us and support us. And it's great that you make sure we have the team we need, but you are the bottleneck when projects get delayed. We're not letting YOU hire another person for this business until you hire someone for yourself."

I didn't have much choice after that. My team held the interviews—which may have been accurately called auditions—until they found the perfect person. The impact of bringing my Strategic Assistant on to the team was so powerful and amazing that even my children noticed. I recently overheard my daughter tell her, "Thank you for helping our dad; life would be so crazy around here without you."

Many push back on putting this person in place because it requires entrepreneurs to be open and transparent about everything in their businesses as well as much of their personal lives. We set ourselves and our assistants up for failure when we give them "as needed" information or hire based on thinking of it as a cost rather than an investment.

After you make the decision to hire an assistant, you may be tempted to keep it as low budget as possible. Some try Virtual Assistants first. However, this is not the same as having an in-person or even a remote Executive Assistant. A Virtual Assistant handles tasks on an assigned basis. They repeat the same actions over and over again, unable to see the big picture or think strategically.

The Executive Assistant, even a remote one, becomes the leader in the relationship. You might be the boss, but when you hire the correct person, you no longer take the lead. She knows the goals for the company as well as your personal life and puts you in a position to meet them.

To avoid setting yourself up for failure, you need an Executive Assistant who truly understands the company's goals as well as your personal aspirations. This person knows what your perfect day looks like—not just the nine-to-five, but also your habits before and after office hours. A core principle of Superpowers is teaching EAs to think of their entrepreneur as a person with limited time, energy, and bandwidth. Goals and milestones become secondary. The primary objective for the EA is their entrepreneur's energy stores—physically, emotionally, and relationally. What will best set them up for success in each of these areas? By creating a structure around the person as much as the needs of the business, the EA brings a win-win to the table because both succeed when everything has balance.

The entrepreneur's nature says yes to every request, opportunity, and relationship without thinking of the cost to the energy supply. And while EAs can't stop every yes, they can delegate and restructure the entrepreneur's calendar to create time, energy, and bandwidth to make sure the scales don't tip too far one way or the other. The entrepreneur who has a balance between their physical, mental, emotional, and spiritual energy has the space to be creative, and that is worth its weight in gold for business growth.

Think about those mundane aspects of your business. How often do you get an email and open it fifteen times before you send the thirty-second reply? We end up touching those little tasks dozens of times before they're completed for one of a dozen reasons. Something more interesting or of higher priority hits our radar, or the email includes a complaint, triggering an emotional reaction that clouds our judgment in choosing a next step or forces us to hold our response until we have time to carefully prepare. Unfortunately, every touch steals a few seconds of our day. Let's face it—most entrepreneurs feel drained when they have to deal with tasks like scheduling, replying to emails, and other tedious yet vital underpinnings of the business.

> I love it that Alice has complete control of my inbox. When I open it, I know every message needs my attention. I used to put off going through email until the weekend, but now I can handle it every day.
>
> —Bo Barron, Barron Commercial Group

At Strategic Coach and Superpowers, we meet with people every day who feel as though they're damaging their own business. They've discovered they can't be all things at all times. Still, despite the fact they are mentally exhausted from working outside their own superpower and they know they need an intervention, they have more than a few objections, fears, and holdbacks.

Most Common Objections to Having an Executive Assistant

Most of the objections to hiring an Executive Assistant fall in the realm of self-limiting beliefs and setting yourself up for failure. While this list is anything but exhaustive, see if one or two resonate with you.

- Do I really deserve an EA?
- Have I earned the right to have an Executive Assistant?
- Is my business big enough to merit an EA?
- How will people perceive me if I have a personal Executive Assistant?
- Adding an Executive Assistant is too expensive.
- How will I see a Return on Investment?
- The benefits don't outweigh the risks.
- I don't have the time to train and manage an Executive Assistant.
- An Executive Assistant won't understand my business.
- I'm concerned about the Executive Assistant's ability to communicate effectively.
- I'm worried the Executive Assistant won't be able to integrate with my existing workflows and processes.
- I'm worried my team will resent this person and feel as though they don't have the same direct access to me.
- I'm concerned about privacy and data security.
- I'm worried they'll resent my free time or my lifestyle.
- I'm not sure this will improve my bottom line.
- How will the Executive Assistant handle sensitive information?

Each one of these mental battles will ultimately undermine the relationship before it even begins.

Shannon's Hesitation

Almost every time I hired someone to support me directly, my anxiety level rose, and I started doubting myself. *Do I have enough work to fill their time? Am I really worth this investment?* (Because that's honestly what it was—an investment in me!) And because I was paying someone a healthy income, it made me take a step back and ask more questions: *Will this hire free up my creativity and productivity enough to generate way more than their salary? What's the business case scenario behind the need?* "Am I worth it?" may have been the biggest question I had to overcome.

Then, there's all the doubt surrounding a new teamwork relationship. I was pretty confident in my abilities, but before I connected with the right person, I'd been burned a couple of times with people I didn't connect or blend well with. So, that caused some nervousness, which I call scar tissue.

Finally, the frustration factor became bigger than the doubt. I think that is probably what propels most people. They either get a push from someone like Steven's team or figure out they are the bottleneck. They say, "Enough! I just have to take the plunge and see if I can make it work."

I can't truly explain all the benefits of taking the risk. Adding a full-time Strategic Assistant just for me has made more difference than words can express. I feel like I got so very lucky. Now, I can't imagine life without her.

And when we begin to explain the expanded role of an Executive Assistant, even more questions and concerns arise:

- I'm concerned about the Executive Assistant's level of expertise.
- I'm worried the Executive Assistant won't be as invested in my business.
- I'm concerned about the Executive Assistant's ability to handle complex tasks.
- I'm worried the Executive Assistant won't be able to prioritize tasks effectively.
- I'm worried the Executive Assistant won't be able to handle emergencies or urgent requests.
- I'm concerned about the Executive Assistant's ability to handle complex scheduling and travel arrangements.
- I'm concerned about the Executive Assistant's ability to handle high-level strategic tasks.

While each of these objections has merit, the three of us represent only a minuscule percentage of entrepreneurs who will attest to the way an Executive Assistant has taken them off the seesaw and allowed them to experience both freedom and growth.

What you're about to read isn't a "how-to" manual or a sales pitch; it's a deep dive into the uncharted territories of the entrepreneur/Executive Assistant relationship. We hope these raw, gritty, and real teamwork stories fuel mindset shifts and rally you—the entrepreneur—to forge next-level partnerships with an EA. Allow the experience of others to spark innovation and bold moves that unlock new levels of freedom and growth.

As you read, we encourage you to envision your perfect day. Write down everything you could accomplish if you had a day with no distractions. And when you've finished, ask yourself what gets in the way of perfection. Then, turn the page and get ready for an honest, no-nonsense blueprint that will revolutionize your entrepreneurial journey and give you the freedom to be Superpowered.

My Perfect Day

Takeaways

1. The EA is the entrepreneur's Stage Manager. They organize everything and pass to you only what is necessary to make the production (your business) a success.
2. Find an EA with the right skills and an entrepreneurial mindset who understands your communication style. They can help close loops in your brain and delegate and restructure your calendar to create time, energy, and bandwidth.
3. Stress and confusion increase your self-limiting beliefs, which compound as you're forced to work harder outside your Unique Ability—the result can become debilitating.
4. Select an assistant who truly understands the company's goals as well as your personal aspirations. A Virtual Assistant handles tasks on an assigned basis, while an Executive Assistant, even a remote one, becomes the leader in the relationship.
5. Allow the experience of others to spark innovation and bold moves that unlock new levels of freedom and growth.

PART TWO

Supershift

If you don't have an executive assistant,
you are one.

—Cameron Herald

As Essential as Food

If you look good, you feel good,
If you feel good, you play good,
If you play good, they pay good

—Deion Sanders
Eight-time Pro Bowler, nine-time All pro,
and two-time Super Bowl champion

A growth mindset may be the number one sign of an entrepreneur on the road to success. Without this key trait, even the most brilliant idea has little chance. The most creative men and women continually watch for new strategies and opportunities for personal and professional growth. And when we see the growth process as difficult or painful, we subconsciously stifle our potential.

When business leaders talk about adding a personal support person, they frame it as an indulgence. Those with this luxury mindset still live in the bottom half of the Superpowered Scale. Yet, for many, one section of their thinking gets partitioned off. In their quest for expansion, growth, and freedom for their family and their business, they often neglect themselves. They spend money to support their team and continually look for ways to provide value to their clients. However, when they talk about adding a personal support person, they frame it as an indulgence. Those with this luxury mindset still live in the bottom half of the Superpowered Scale. They struggle and trudge along even when the business that began as their passion becomes drudgery.

> **When business leaders talk about adding a personal support person, they frame it as an indulgence. Those with this luxury mindset still live in the bottom half of the Superpowered Scale.**

To shift the mindset of having personal support from extravagance to essential, consider how oil affects your car's engine. While everything can technically move without it, the lubricant reduces friction and ensures all the gears and pistons work seamlessly. Those who neglect this vital component discover its importance when they find themselves stranded alongside the road or paying for repairs on a blown engine. Similarly, an Executive Assistant helps reduce the friction of daily tasks. By managing the flow of information and ensuring everything operates smoothly, the entrepreneur can focus on strategic decisions and high-ticket activities. In many cases, like oil does for the engine, the EA allows the entrepreneur to be productive and enjoy his position for years longer than those who ignore the signs.

Living in Your Unique Ability

Think about the effects of depriving your body of the essential nutrients we get from food. Without protein, we get tired and can develop bone diseases. A lack of vegetables has been known to lead to cancer, stroke, and heart disease. Without food, we will eventually quit breathing. And devoid of an Executive Assistant, you will start to feel like you can't breathe.

Strategic Coach says, "At the core of your being are characteristics and values entirely unique to you." They call these characteristics and values your Unique Ability, traits that drive you to your purpose. And some say when they find a way to work in this niche that makes them uncommonly special, the labor comes as naturally as breathing.

Shannon's Struggle

I started with one assistant who was shared among three people. So, I never had her full attention or focus. Because there were three of us, she couldn't possibly match us all personality-wise. Looking back, I feel bad for the stress she must have had switching personalities every time she walked into someone else's office. It didn't really work out well and added to my resistance.

Work was a struggle. I had so much to get done, and many of the activities I needed to complete, I just wasn't good at, which meant they really slowed me down. Obviously, I started with the things I was good at. So, I felt like I got all my fun work done really fast and then was left with the boring, hard stuff. I ended up working late at night to get everything done.

> Strategic Coach has a rule about Free Days: they run a full twenty-four hours, midnight to midnight. I can't count the nights I worked till 11:59 pm so I could get a great Free Day and not push those boundaries too much. But it was hard, and doing all that work, I had no business doing made me mentally exhausted. I felt like I had hit a plateau in terms of how much I could grow. I didn't have the time or capacity to do more, so my future was limited.

Too often, entrepreneurs and business leaders get caught up in the little things. Stuck in the muck of details outside their innate abilities, they find their energy drained. However, life doesn't have to be that way. Each person possesses a unique set of skills or characteristics that actually fuel us when we use them. Your Unique Ability is the very essence of what makes you "you." Still, few can articulate the source of what empowers them—another reason to take time to describe your ideal day.

When you live in your Unique Ability, your productivity automatically soars because you enjoy what you're doing. Even if you aren't certain what that ability is, you've probably been doing some task—perhaps a task others find tedious—and lost track of time. You become so engrossed in the project that nothing exists outside of it.

Until your phone dings and you need to answer an email.

Or someone calls, and you have to schedule a meeting.

Or your calendar reminder signals it's time to stop what you're doing and prepare your notes for tomorrow's meeting, and you don't even know where all the information is to prepare, and while you're searching for the information, you discover you missed an appointment because you didn't have the reminder set right.

Although life felt simple and beautiful just two minutes ago, you now feel like someone has his hands around your neck choking you.

But what if you had an Executive Assistant to take care of those emails and calendar dates? How would your life change if you had a support person who gathered everything you needed to prepare for tomorrow's meeting? How much time would you save, and how much of that time could you spend being creative?

> Email and Social Media are the places where all productivity goes to die. I'm thankful to my Executive Assistant for keeping me out of the purgatory and on track to the promised land!
> –Steven Neuner

You might call all those distractions drudgery and feel bad passing them off to someone else; however, in the capable hands of the right assistant, one person's drudgery is another's thirty-second challenge. You see, when you engage an Executive Assistant who has unique abilities exactly opposite yours, everything you find draining now fuels someone else's Unique Ability. They're actually excited to take on the task you saw as a heavyweight. An Executive Assistant allows you to move faster and more confidently because you're doing the things you love while your assistant takes on the tasks that give them energy. And because everyone is 10xing their task list, productivity skyrockets.

> ### Shannon's Dread is Katrina's Tetris
>
> I hate scheduling. Even putting one event on the calendar drains my energy. But I love watching Katrina. Scheduling is actually fun for her—she describes it as playing a game of Tetris. And my last assistant told me she used scheduling as a way to calm down. I can't even imagine handling a calendar with that attitude, but I'm grateful Katrina is there to take care of it for me.

Strategic Coach and Superpowers both put a great deal of stock in the work of Kolbe Corp. They stress the importance of focusing your mental energy on the area of your greatest strengths. While the Kolbe Index focuses on the ways we strive and problem solve rather than using our unique characters and abilities, when we apply their philosophy of each person conserving his or her mental energy by working within their innate traits, we see increased productivity and peace of mind.

An Executive Assistant – What It's Not

Before we go any further in unveiling the secret of the Executive Assistant's Superpower, let's stop for a moment and clear up some misconceptions. First, your Executive Assistant will not be your clone. You might enjoy the interview more with someone who shares your characteristics and abilities; however, if you hire your clone, you'll end up living in Supershift Level Two of the Superpowered Scale. Frustration will set in because your new hire ends up doing all the things you love to do and can't accomplish the tasks you hate any better than you. In fact, they want your job.

Second, your Executive Assistant should never be your dumping ground, nor should any person on your team. Simply delegating your least favorite tasks will only take you as far as Supershift Level Three. You'll never make it to the top. You want someone whose Unique Ability complements yours in every way. If you hate jigsaw puzzles, the person you hire should love them. The more members of your team—including your Executive Assistant—you empower to live in their Unique Ability, the faster you can exponentially increase productivity, freedom, growth, and joy in your company.

The 3Ps Framework[IP] shows us the three distinctly different levels of assistants that are often mistakenly grouped together:

- **Project Assistant.** If you have a long-term project, you might bring an extra person—part-time or full-time—onto your team. For instance, someone dedicated to recording and editing your podcast or managing your website. These specialists complete narrowly focused tasks with a clear objective. They'll create graphics or logos or write content for your marketing. The Project Assistant has specific skills to move the project forward.
- Many confuse a **Process Assistant** with an Executive Assistant. This person provides consistent execution of a known and defined step-by-step process. Answering phones, filing, and delivering mail fall into these categories. For predictable processes, a virtual assistant can be helpful because the person needs no creativity or critical analysis skills.
- An Executive Assistant is not confined to projects or processes. This elite role is a **Proactive Assistant.** She develops a high-level relationship with the entrepreneur and keeps all the pieces moving in the

entrepreneur's life. Many entrepreneurs become wary about adding an Executive Assistant because they've had Project and Process Assistants in the past and don't understand the vast differences.

What an Executive Assistant Is

What if you had a proactive assistant who analyzed your energy levels throughout the day to determine when you were most productive and scheduled accordingly? How would your life change if this person blocked out time on your calendar for focused work within your Unique Ability, as well as breaks that allowed you to recharge and stay energized? And if this person had the authority to remove all distractions and interruptions so you could delve into your passion for hours at a time and allocate time for personal development, how much time would you save?

> With an assistant, you don't have to worry about pain points anymore because someone you trust is handling them better than you could. —Jacob Emery, R&R Pipeline, Inc.

Does that sound too good to be true?

Superpowers and Strategic Coach see this scenario play out every day. And those criteria are just a few from the Superpowers' "Ideal Week Playbook[IP]." You see, while you manage the company, the EA manages you. You might be the boss, but she becomes the leader. When Superpowers matches Executive Assistants with entrepreneurs, we find people with the Unique Ability to get to know you, understand you, and ultimately anticipate you. This person pulls you forward and moves proactively on your behalf. And while this thought makes some entrepreneurs nervous at first, every single one learns to love that their Executive Assistant speaks for them. The entire team, as well as clients, come to learn your EA is your proxy.

An Executive Assistant doesn't serve the company; she serves you. The only project she manages is the entrepreneur, and she manages every aspect—time, energy, and attention. Strategic Coach tells assistants, "Your entrepreneur is your Focus Activity." Because of this prioritization, the EA helps make certain the entrepreneur can operate within his or her Unique Ability at least eighty percent of the time. With an Executive Assistant managing you, you will finally feel as though you can breathe again.

Celeena Manages Steven

I guess the word will get out now. Celeena manages my social media presence. When I go in there to check on my friends, I get sucked down the rabbit hole of all the posts that don't matter. I want to know what's going on in my friends' lives, but I can't risk opening the platforms. Before Celeena, I missed a friend's wedding because the invite came through Facebook, and I was trying to avoid the time suck.

Every week, Celeena gives me a social media update on anyone in my closest friends list. At Superpowers, we call this The Better Friend Report™. She includes pictures and posts, so I see every important event in the lives of these people who are significant to me. She replies with my response on my behalf so my friends know I care, and she adds their e-vites to my calendar. Celeena even helps me send gifts when someone shares pictures of their new baby or a recent move. I don't miss a thing, but I don't lose productivity by clicking on things that slow me down.

In their book *Who Not How,* Dr. Benjamin Hardy and Dan Sullivan take us deep into the Strategic Coach principle of hiring the right person. Rather than looking for our clone or someone to manage our projects or processes, we need to define the person who will make our lives easier.

We tend to ask questions that begin with the word "how"—"How can I accomplish this goal?" However, the correct question, the one that will propel us forward, is "Who can help me accomplish this goal?" or "Who can reach this goal for me?" We ask you to consider, "Who has the Unique Ability to take over everything that keeps you from working in your Unique Ability?"

When we put the correct "Who" in place, we become tremendously productive. And the Executive Assistant thrives seeing the entrepreneur achieve their personal and professional goals. Their unique abilities allow their bosses to show up and be their best selves. The partnership allows everything the entrepreneurs were doing on their own to get done better than ever before. It's difficult to continually deliver at the level you expect of yourself when you're running a business—especially when you have a to-do list filled with tasks you're not good at. However, a phenomenal EA with the right Unique Ability can keep you focused and headed in the right direction. They also unlock success in all parts of entrepreneurs' lives. Not only can the entrepreneur cast the vision and be their best for the company, they can give their best to their families. Days off bring the rest and rejuvenation the entrepreneur needs.

The highly skilled Executive Assistant works for more than just a paycheck. We like to call these priceless individuals the hidden 10x factors in every entrepreneur's life.

Strategic Coach has more than three decades of evidence that proves one major roadblock preventing entrepreneurs from increasing revenue is the lack of time to think. When these business owners take just four days away to focus their thoughts on how they can change by integrating Coach's solutions, they often double their income. And that's the benefit of just four days a year without an EA to provide scheduling support.

By taking time to think about their relationships, how they are managing their money and their time, how they are fulfilling their purpose, and what they're doing to improve their health and well-being, entrepreneurs can be more intentional with their efforts. These men and women are tremendous at keeping busy and working hard; however, great Executive Assistants learn early the value of scheduling time for their entrepreneurs to take a break from their striving so they can just think.

From Burnout to Boom

Both of our organizations, Strategic Coach and Superpowers, encounter entrepreneurs in the Resignation and Desperation phases of the Superpowered Scale—zones born of burnout. You can only max out your mental energy for so long before you implode. Superpowers trains EAs to recognize the stages of burnout after trust and communication have been established. This is one of the reasons having someone who complements you is vital. If your EA is your clone, they will have the same blind spots you do. But an EA trained to protect you and set you up for success will see burnout as a threat to guard against. They know to watch for the weeks when you begin to misplace blame or your behavior changes. Your EA will see when you begin to neglect yourself so you never fall into the most destructive areas of burnout. We've included our *12 Stages of Burnout Guide*[IP] on the SuperpoweredBook.com resource page so you and your Executive Assistant can identify the signs.

If you've ever been part of Strategic Coach, you probably can't count the number of times you've heard the term Free Days. The most successful business leaders understand that without an opportunity to rejuvenate and refuel, they will run out of steam.

Perhaps you've continued to operate your vehicle after the oil light comes on. If so, you know the friction and heat created by the gears and wheels rubbing together without oil causes serious problems. As we noted before, without basic maintenance, you will find yourself sitting alongside the road with a blown engine.

Entrepreneurs face the same kind of disaster if they don't find what they need to fuel their tanks and grease the wheels. Their knee-jerk reaction is to hire someone exactly like them. They want a replica so they can get off the treadmill. The entrepreneur just wants the pain to stop. Some resort to employing a high-priced COO; however, if you're still simply throwing them all your work without understanding their unique abilities, you may end up hiring an expensive clone.

A car was made to carry passengers. Likewise, the entrepreneur has an internal drive and purpose that can't be shut off so easily. Hiring in desperation doesn't make the angst better; it simply makes it different.

The right Executive Assistant moves the business leader from burnout to boom. Moving from the tactical help of the Delegation Level to Transformation status means you have someone two steps ahead of you. The Executive Assistant takes care of scheduling and doesn't allow the person they're managing to overbook their lives. We know some EAs who've ordered meals to be delivered because they know their entrepreneur won't stop to find something to eat.

Ryan's First Executive Assistant

I'm not sure how long I would have struggled without an Executive Assistant if my friend, who was also a business owner, hadn't sent Amber to me like a hand-delivered gift. I was buried and drowning under the weight of my business. I knew I needed a life preserver, but the thought of finding the right person was overwhelming.

I had a whole list of questions. *How do I find the right person? How do I train them? What should onboarding look like? What should I expect? How will I know if things are on track?* I know—you have to answer those questions for every role. But you hire an entire team of salespeople or account managers. As the business grows, you just keep adding. I knew I'd have second and third chances to get it right with those positions. However, with an EA, I'd need to find the perfect fit on the first try because I'd only have one, and the thought of having to get it right the first time froze me in my tracks. So, I put it on the back burner. The company required salespeople, but an EA could come in at any time.

By the time Amber came on board, I was missing emails, double booking, showing up late to appointments, and constantly feeling unprepared. The Unique Ability she brought to our team completed what we needed to become the business someone wanted to purchase.

We know the search can be daunting; however, when you find the person who can pick up where you stop and create space in your schedule for family and personal time, you'll see the payoff.

Takeaways

1. An Executive Assistant helps reduce the friction of daily tasks by managing the flow of information and ensuring everything operates smoothly. This allows you to focus on strategic decisions and high-ticket activities.

2. "At the core of your being are characteristics and values entirely unique to you." When you live in your Unique Ability, your productivity automatically soars because you enjoy what you're doing.

3. An Executive Assistant allows you to move faster and more confidently because you're doing the things you love while your assistant takes on the tasks that give him or her energy. Your EA helps make certain you can operate within your Unique Ability at least eighty percent of the time.

4. The more members of your team—including your Executive Assistant—you empower to live in their Unique Ability, the faster you can exponentially increase productivity, freedom, growth, and joy in your company.

5. Without an opportunity to rejuvenate and refuel, you will run out of steam. A trained EA will protect you and set you up for success by identifying when burnout is a threat.

Behind Every Great Entrepreneur

Great vision without great people is irrelevant.

—Jim Collins

Have you ever heard the name Charles Batchelor? The world would not be the same without his tremendous technical skills. He worked with Thomas Edison on the phonograph, electric lighting, and motion pictures, laying a foundation for the comfort and entertainment we enjoy today. You may know the name Watson; however, few understand the significant part he played in Alexander Graham Bell's life or his contribution to communication technology. Did you know Marie Curie had a collaborator while working to isolate and identify radium? She may not have progressed nearly as quickly without the skills of André-Louis Debierne. And what would Henry Ford have done without "Cast Iron

Charlie" Sorenson, who made substantial contributions to the manufacturing process?[1]

History books tend to highlight Edison, Bell, Curie, and Ford, but none of them would have advanced so far alone. And while each of the four mentioned above was considered assistants to the names we learned in high school, those less famed men were really collaborators—experts in their fields—exactly what we need to look for when we begin the search for our Executive Assistant.

While some view the position as a stepping stone or a place of leverage, we passionately believe the right Executive Assistant thinks of themselves as a partner in the operation of the company. Few people have the unique abilities required to be an effective Executive Assistant. This position could be considered the heartbeat of the entrepreneur's success. To truly 10x production, freedom, and growth, every entrepreneur and business leader needs someone who embraces the vital nature of this career choice.

Ensuring the Company Doesn't Implode

Within a few years of adding an Executive Assistant, my free days moved from zero to at least one hundred fifty-five each year.
—Steven Neuner

- What difference would it make to your business if you never again worried about something falling through the cracks?
- How would you spend your time if you never had to face the tyranny of the urgent?

- Are you an entrepreneur as well as a parent? What if you had the ability to never miss another soccer game or concert and didn't feel like you were letting someone else down by being there?
- How would your life change if you found only the most relevant email messages in your inbox?
- How would you feel if you could have at least 155 days out of the office each year without the business imploding?

Do the answers to these questions feel like unattainable aspirations? We are living proof they don't have to be. Plus, we know countless others working in the fullness of their Unique Ability. And the single common denominator is an Executive Assistant.

The right Executive Assistant becomes your partner in business. He or she helps run your life and allows you to see the potential for your future is unlimited. With the right EA in place, your team might not even notice when you're out of the office—even if it's for thirty consecutive days.

Explore Your Options

As we mentioned in the last chapter, depending on the task, you might engage a project assistant or process assistant. These might be temporary or permanent, depending on your business and the types of services you provide. However, if you want to grow your business and have the freedom to stay active in what you love to do most, you will need an entre-preneurial Executive Assistant.

The biggest dilemma most entrepreneurs face when they finally shift their mindset to realize the necessity of an Executive Assistant is whether this person should work in person or remotely. Second, should you hire a personal Executive Assistant or a shared resource?

Historically, business leaders felt they needed an in-person assistant. The old mindset presents many objections to hiring a remote Executive Assistant.

- I'm worried a remote Executive Assistant won't be able to build strong relationships with my team.
- I'm concerned about a remote Executive Assistant's reliability and availability.
- I don't know how I would monitor a remote Executive Assistant. How can I be sure the person is really doing the work?

Honestly, after you hire your assistant, even if he or she is in your office every day, you'll discover they're remote to you. This person will set you free from your desk. If you enjoy getting out and talking to clients and customers, you will only be in the office when it's absolutely necessary. Leaders who offer services in industries that need speakers will find themselves flying all over the world to share their products and messages. If you work better in complete silence, you may find out your home office gives you more peace than coming in and facing the entire team every day. Whatever the reason, many entrepreneurs discover they communicate with their assistants more over a messaging service or phone than face-to-face—even if the assistant comes into the office daily.

Requiring an in-person assistant also trims your hiring pool. No one wants to drive more than thirty to forty-five minutes to get to the office. Even in the largest metropolitan setting, you exponentially reduce the number of candidates and will probably miss the one who is uniquely suited to your personality, business, and team. Consider the vast difference in the number of candidates you'll find in a thirty-mile radius of your office compared to the number of resumes you might get from across the US or around the world.

Superpowers finds matches for business leaders in the Philippines. And while some worry about the time difference or language barrier, we've found extremely skilled individuals excited to use their unique abilities. They speak fluent English and accommodate your time zone. Most importantly, they don't look down on the Executive Assistant role as a stepping stone. Rather, they recognize it for what it is: an esteemed position worthy of a career. If you close your mind to a remote assistant, you cheat yourself out of thousands of tremendous candidates.

Some start out hiring an Executive Assistant as a shared resource. They think they can't afford their own; however, often, this excuse just masks their guilt about hiring someone whose primary role is to support them. Many worry they'll look selfish or their team will think they don't want to work hard. Others become concerned other members of their team will resent them or think less of their tenacity and willingness to do what it takes to be successful. But as Shannon told us earlier, this has a number of drawbacks. It's difficult to find someone who will fit more than one personality, and the situation has the potential to overwhelm the assistant because no one but the assistant knows how much the other leaders ask her to do.

Honestly, you self-sabotage when you choose the shared resource option. We know some of you feel guilty just thinking about being the only one in the office with an EA. This becomes another necessary mindset shift. The freedom you experience with an Executive Assistant will benefit the entire team. You will be more present for them, and the business will naturally grow. But unless you set clear boundaries, each team member in the office will ask the assistant to do "just one little thing" until the little things keep your poor assistant way past quitting time. Before long, she won't be able to work in her Unique Ability any more than you were before you hired her. Because you're hiring a professional with a proactive and helpful personality, she will be more than willing to take on those extra jobs. Soon, you'll have yourself a burned-out assistant.

Shannon's Shared Assistant

I started with a shared part-time assistant. However, at one point, my colleague decided she wanted to hire someone independent. I had to make a decision, and fear held me up for a while. I only had access to her about ten hours a week, so I honestly didn't think I had enough work for her. But I hated to let her go. I deliberated for a while but finally kept her as my personal Executive Assistant. It only took me three weeks to realize having an assistant devoted to me was a complete game changer—so much so that I asked her how soon she could go full-time!

Because I had her to myself, my productivity skyrocketed, and I gave her more and more of my responsibilities—things she was really good at. She was instrumental in the company's success. It was amazing!

Today, I hand my email, scheduling, and organizing over to Katrina—my personal manager and support partner. She takes my ideas, shapes them, and adds awesome input. Plus, she gently reminds me of what I need to be doing—she keeps me on task. Once you've had a taste of what an Executive Assistant can do for you and your business, there's no turning back.

The Secret (Or Not So Secret) Formula

Strategic Coach introduces every participant to The 4 C's Formula®: Commitment, Courage, Capability, and Confidence. Hiring an Executive Assistant opens the door to a 4Cs moment every time. It requires Commitment to something new, which triggers the Courage to move forward. Taking the first step allows you to feel more Capable, and finding the right candidate will give you Confidence so that it will be a little easier the next time.

But, after you've made the Commitment and drummed up the Courage, how do you get the Capability to find the perfect Executive Assistant, especially if you've been burned a few times before?

First, you need to know yourself. When we shared Eric's story earlier, you may have noticed that one of his biggest problems was that he needed someone to tell him how smart he was. Clarity

> I should never be part of the first round of hiring. I'm a really good salesperson, which means I work to sell someone on the job whether they are the right fit or not. —Shannon Waller

allows us to make the most profitable commitments. If you are great at sales, you might be tempted to talk anyone into taking the position because you're driven to convince people to like what you're selling. In that case, you probably want someone else on your team to screen the candidates before you talk to them. You also need to know what tasks you love and which ones you need to give up.

Additionally, take a minute to identify the few jobs you need to relinquish but tend to be protective of. We all have a few. If you don't know yourself and your unique abilities, finding the right person to support and manage you will be difficult.

We appreciate Kolbe Corp's work in helping find matches. Someone who is 'long' on the Kolbe Follow Through continuum makes for a great place to start. These folks thrive on highly developed organizational processes. They'll have the mental energy to take care of your calendar, sort through your email, and put your piles into cohesive order. You'll also want to look for someone with numbers at least slightly different than yours. If you are an Initiating Quick Start—and most entrepreneurs tend to fall there—you'll probably want someone whose bar is shorter on the continuum.

Shannon's Kolbe Index

My first assistant, Nicole, had Kolbe MO that showed she was Initiating in Fact Finder and Follow Through with an Accommodating 4 in Quick Start. I'm a nine in Quick Start. We were not the same, and I really didn't want a huge amount of tension. I had to embrace the fact she would compliment me, and since her Quick Start number fell in the middle of the continuum, I knew that she wouldn't completely resist my new ideas. It ended up being fun!

Superpowers uses a proven technique to match business leaders with assistants. First, we talk to the entrepreneur to determine his or her needs and get a feel for the culture of the company. Then, we interview about a hundred candidates to narrow the field to a manageable group and find the perfect fit. That number shocks many of our clients; however, experience tells us that's what's needed to find the person who can manage you and fit your business perfectly.

The process begins with a series of questions and a web recording that quickly eliminates the applicants who won't work for a particular client. This is followed by two face-to-face web meetings to go deeper. Finally, we provide a small portion of the interviewees with a week of training, during which they also work on mock projects to see how they handle managing a calendar and emails, making independent decisions, and working autonomously.

This is a rigorous and intense process, but we've found it's one that brings consistent long-term success. Every step has been designed and refined based on our experience of identifying elite Executive Assistants. We count it a victory when we can match a client with an assistant who exceeds their expectations and becomes a long-time part of their team.

Executive Assistants hold a truly unique position. These individuals have the ability to keep up with the growth-minded business leader. This means the screening process takes a bit more finesse than any other hire in the company. For instance, we present trainees with real-life scenarios like this one to evaluate their problem-solving skills:

What would you do if your boss called you at noon to say he was heading into a meeting and would not be available for calls until after five? At the same time, he needs a flight home at six.

The chances of finding the right flight at exactly 6:00 p.m. will be rare. A good candidate for Executive Assistant makes the decision without consulting the business leader or his spouse. Will she book the 5:30 p.m. flight or the 7:00 p.m. flight? You want an EA who thinks independently and takes action.

The best candidates work proactively. They don't stop with booking a flight. Our best applicants suggest creating a short list of places to eat dinner on the way to the airport and contacting the entrepreneur's family with the approximate wheels-down time. Even in the interview process, the most creative candidates float to the top with their thoughtfulness and care.

Part of the Superpowers' Discovery Process includes exploring their past success. Many entrepreneurs get stuck trying to define this new role, but after they draw on their experience, they find it easier to describe the ultimate mix of characteristics that will make the relationship successful.

When looking for an assistant, think about all the people you've worked well with. What are some common characteristics of the people you feel most productive with? When working closely with someone, what personality traits bring you the most joy? Create a detailed list below and use this as a springboard to fuel your search.

My List of Great People to Work With	Characteristics

Shannon Needs Someone Smart

Maybe one of the reasons I recognized what Eric needed was because that's what I needed too. I knew if Eric didn't find someone who could keep up with him mentally, he would plummet on the Superpowered Scale. The only things that come from hiring someone who doesn't challenge us intellectually are frustration and resignation.

To identify someone who fits that description, I ask why they left their last position. Both Nicole and Katrina came to me after learning their previous role so thoroughly that they got bored. Intelligent people need constant stimulation and input, something entrepreneurs are uniquely suited to providing.

I've never had anyone get bored working with me! I always have new and interesting projects, so neither of my wonderful Support Partners ever had to worry about being bored again!

Yes, it takes time and diligence to find the perfect match. Fortunately, when you find the right person, the benefits make you feel like you found the big X on the treasure map.

The Ideal Assistant

Every entrepreneur and business leader needs an Executive Assistant with an entrepreneurial mindset. At Strategic Coach, we've created a resource called the Entrepreneurial Attitude Exercise to help you identify candidates with this important asset. The best EAs love the fact they get to be in an entrepreneurial setting without the pressure of actually being the entrepreneur. These individuals thrive on seeing a job well done, and their rare combination of organizational savvy and strategic thinking puts them in a position to empower everyone to do their best work. You'll see just how much they enjoy their positions when you read each of our EAs takes on their roles.

Another important asset is a growth mindset. It's something Superpowers evaluates during the interview process. We have thousands of pages of content and hours of video to train someone to be a stellar EA, but we can not train someone to have a growth mindset. Either you have it, or you don't.

Entrepreneurs are programmed this way. They know every tomorrow will be bigger than today—bigger clients, bigger opportunities, and bigger challenges. In order to go on this journey with you, your Executive Assistant must have this same growth mindset.

Traditional secretaries create transactional relationships in the office. Their day revolves around specific duties listed in a job description. They see entrepreneurial growth as a bigger workload, which creates anxiety because each new item increases the possibility of mistakes.

That's why the ideal Executive Assistant needs this unique mindset. Without it, the trajectories of the partnership diverge. The EA-entrepreneur partnership goes beyond the transactional relationship into what we call a transformational relationship. It would be difficult to wrap up every task she completes in a pretty list.

The Executive Assistant genuinely cares for your well-being, and that care goes both ways. In fact, this relationship opens the door just a bit wider than for any other team member. While it may be a bit uncomfortable at first, this personal aspect makes all the difference. You can hire an

IT guy and never have a personal relationship with him; you might think of him more as a commodity. The Executive Assistant will never fall into that category. This is a transformative relationship that even your family and friends will appreciate.

Getting to know one another on a more personal level is a critical building block that will make your business strong. Relationships in which the executives keep their EAs at arm's length nearly always fizzle out within six months. Contrast that to the teams still going strong after six years and have taken the time to develop this important aspect.

Perhaps you're one of the numerous entrepreneurs and business leaders who feel sapped of mental energy. Working outside of your Unique Ability and innate strengths drains you. The ideal assistant takes those jobs that steal your mental energy and completes them in less than half the time. Because she's working in the area of her natural strengths, these vital elements of the business don't tax her mental capabilities. This means she has a mental reserve to do even more, and you get to do the things that fuel your brain. And if that wasn't enough, she shares her mental energy. This complementary personality brings activities and ideas to the partnership you would never think of on your own.

If you talk to the most successful entrepreneurs—not the ones with the most money, the ones with the most freedom and growth—you'll find an Executive Assistant of some kind in the wings. You'll also discover the transition isn't always smooth. We've discovered the process has a few traps to watch out for along the way.

Takeaways

1. Right EAs think of themselves as partners and become your partner in operating the business. They help run your life and allow you to see that your future potential is unlimited.

2. The freedom you experience with an EA—as opposed to a project assistant or process assistant—will benefit the entire team. You will be more present for them, and the business will naturally grow.

3. You want an EA who thinks independently, takes action, and works proactively.

4. The best EAs love being in an entrepreneurial setting without the pressure of actually being the entrepreneur. They thrive on seeing a job well done, and their rare combination of organizational savvy and strategic thinking puts them in a position to empower everyone to do their best work. Having a growth mindset is a huge part of this.

5. The EA-entrepreneur partnership goes beyond the transactional relationship into a transformational relationship. Getting to know one another on a more personal level is a critical building block that will make your business strong.

Don't Pick the Lock

If hard work is the key to success,
most people would rather pick the lock.

—Claude MacDonald

Entrepreneurs tend to have a "ready to change the world and make it a better place" mindset. They naturally challenge the status quo. You might be amazed at the similarity of entrepreneurs and the things that trip them up. We consistently hear the same stories when people begin talking about what prevents them from achieving their ambitions and realizing their vision for the future of their businesses, their families, and the world.

Taking the leap to hire your first Executive Assistant can feel a lot like standing at the door of an airplane, ready to skydive for the first time. You don't know exactly what to expect, and the endeavor seems costly and risky. Plus, as we've said, finding the right fit can take time and hard work. Unfortunately, many spend years trying to pick the lock.

Perhaps you're thinking, *It's just easier to do it myself,* or *will adding an Executive Assistant truly pay for itself?*

Many have those thoughts and more, but the ones who shifted their mindsets will tell you that the view from the mountaintop was well worth the decision and commitment it took to get there.

We understand you are highly intelligent and capable of doing just about anything you set your mind to. Entrepreneurs have that knack. We know how to create workarounds, and we are fast learners. Why would we farm out the jobs we can do ourselves? We already invest in specialists for graphics, websites, marketing, and other highly skilled needs.

But what if someone who can manage your time, eliminate the suck, and give you 10x impact is that same kind of investment?

Ryan's Take on Trying to Do It All

I feel like we're just fooling ourselves if we think we can do everything on our own. One of the biggest mistakes entrepreneurs make is not seeing those daily repeating tasks as a specialist's role. We are not the right person to eliminate the suck. Too many times, we're the ones creating it! One of the most powerful mindset shifts is acknowledging we're fundamentally not good at these things. Even if we're able to do them, we'll never be awesome at them.

Unfortunately, some who step out of their comfort zone to hire an Executive Assistant still fall prey to some of the traps and pitfalls of moving forward. Bringing a personal manager into your team requires a mental supershift that can be difficult for micro-managers.

Delegate Up

If you're considering hiring an Executive Assistant, one major pre-qualification is the business leader's willingness to relinquish control of their calendar and inbox. This is a deal-breaker for many entrepreneurs. However, the relationship will be a disappointment if you attempt to shortcut this mindset. Think about the hours you spend deleting spam and unnecessary messages. Consider how many times you had to go back and forth with your last contact before you nailed the date for your meeting.

It's great to not have to go back and forth with folks trying to find time to schedule meetings. My EA is a Superpower, freeing me up to get more work done instead of scheduling!
–Jason Ganahl, GQue BBQ

Some entrepreneurs have a difficult time giving up these little tasks. They believe they can handle the small things. Others feel as though they're delegating down, giving menial tasks to someone with extraordinary skills. However, delegating down implies you're passing off work to someone who can't handle more than the one task we give him. We need to shift our mindset to think of turning over these tasks as delegating up. Yes, your assistant has tremendous abilities, and anytime you pass along a job that falls in that skill set, you delegate up. When you get to the end of the book and hear the way our EAs describe their roles, you'll understand the mindset shift you need to make. Instead of viewing the jobs we give our assistants as menial, we need to look at them as meaningful.

The fact is, if your business is growing, you already know how to do this to some extent. Every entrepreneur or leader who experiences growth already understands the process:

- Create a new thing
- Do the new thing
- Grow the new thing
- Hand off the new thing
- Rinse and repeat

The problem with the thought of an EA is the lack of separation. It's not like training someone in sales and sending them off to their department. You are the EA's department. This means you have to develop a level of trust to create security in your collaboration.

Shannon Hears from Frustrated EAs

In Strategic Coach's Strategic Assistant program, we hear the frustration that EAs feel when their entrepreneurs keep a "Delegation Death Grip" on tasks.

Consider what a relay race would look like if you refused to let go of the baton when you reached the next runner. Your team would lose every time, and your teammates would soon try to find a replacement. When the entrepreneur puts off, delays, and procrastinates in areas the Executive Assistant does well, it creates the same kind of friction. Even if it's just tidying up the office, Unique Ability Teamwork means having the courage to let go because your assistant can do the job faster and easier.

Giving your Executive Assistant control doesn't mean you won't see any more emails—unless you don't want to. It does mean you see only the most pertinent messages. For decades, secretaries have been vetting paper mail for executives. Advertisements and unnecessary correspondence either end up in the trash or are taken care of by the secretary without a thought from the person in charge. Assistants of all types have been screening phone calls for at least as long—only calls from clients and close family and friends get forwarded. Why does the thought of your inbox being treated the same way freak you out?

Executive Assistants quickly learn which emails they should reply to on your behalf and which they should leave for you. Best of all, you will never again see a barrage of meaningless messages.

Steven's First Executive Assistant

When my team at the insurance agency brought their choices for my assistant, one stood out. At her interview, she hit the fax machine with her purse and joked about being disqualified for faxing China. Not only was she fun, but she was also incredibly humble. While she didn't tell us at first, over time, I found out she had been a missionary in Chile—her two children were born there. And she had toured and sung with a Contemporary Christian band called *Truth*, which included a concert for the President of the United States!

Fern did more than manage my email and calendar. Because she was highly intentional with every action, I knew each task I gave her was a delegation up. She participated as a key stakeholder in keeping my personal and professional vision for a bigger future for myself and our team. I gave her permission to hold me accountable to core values and to live into my vision. I honestly shared my fears, procrastinations, certainties, uncertainties, and more. This helped her look around corners for me and truly support me.

She blocked time for me to complete Impact Filters™, a key Strategic Coach thinking tool, so I could clarify my most important ideas and prepare for critical meetings. She scheduled collision courses so I couldn't procrastinate on things I wanted to avoid, giving me momentum. Every time I attended Strategic Coach, I came back with new insights. She knew I needed time to process everything, so my schedule always had blocked out hours the day after I returned, and then she helped me turn them into action.

Some entrepreneurs and business leaders struggle to decide what to delegate and what they can't bear to part with. If you're among those who hold tight to the baton, we're guessing you are drowning in your to-do list right now.

Don't Clean Before the Housekeeper Comes

It's difficult to wrap our brains around the fact that just because we think some of the tasks on our list are the crappiest jobs in the company, not everyone sees them that way. We've heard of people putting off hiring an Executive Assistant because their office is too disorganized. "It's just not fair to bring someone in and make them face this mess."

If that's your mindset, you probably clean the house before the housekeeper comes.

People with the personality for the Executive Assistant position thrive on organizing. They see the stacks of papers on your desk as a challenge, not the most dreadful part of their job.

Steven Gets a Front Row Seat to a Change in Mindset

One entrepreneur we know spent a good bit of time researching CRMs. He wanted to have the right software in place before he hired his assistant. He must have asked half a dozen people for their opinions before he got to me.

"I'm trying to get a good CRM in place before my new assistant comes on board. What do you recommend?" He asked.

I asked him a question in return: "Why would you pick a system that someone else is going to have to manage?"

He almost fell out of his chair. He wanted everything to be perfect before his new team member arrived and didn't even think about the fact his new EA might enjoy finding the right CRM software. I still laugh thinking about it.

We've had assistants tell us it pains them to walk by their entrepreneur's messy office. They would go in and clean it if only the entrepreneur would give them permission. The things you don't like to do are probably fun for your Executive Assistant, and lucky for you, she doesn't like to do the things you think are fun.

In this same vein, some don't want to become too dependent on another person. "I don't need someone ordering my lunch. It only takes fifteen minutes." However, multiply that fifteen minutes by at least two hundred fifty work days each year. Is allowing someone to order your food worth sixty-two hours of your time? That seems like a really expensive lunch! Consider, too, that it's nearly impossible to accomplish anything great in life by slicing your day into fifteen-minute chunks. Those who move from one task to another have a difficult time casting a compelling and powerful vision of the future. That fifteen minutes may seem like it's just ordering lunch, but if you're the visionary, does your attitude speak to a broader and more limiting mindset?

That brings us to another mindset shift we have to make in this realm—the belief that because we think the task is "crappy," the person who does the work must be "crappy" too. And who wants to add a "crappy" person to the team? It's time to realize no task is too small—every tiny thing you do is vital to the success of the company. Let's face it: you don't like doing it, so if it weren't important, you wouldn't be doing it.

Additionally, when you put this label on a task—even if it's an offhanded slight—it's a disincentive for someone to raise their hand and volunteer because you've just implied if they like to do it, they must be menial. These items you classify as "crappy" need someone who will view them with the level of respect they deserve. Each of these unbearable tasks should have the touch of someone who possesses the Unique Ability to handle it—usually the Executive Assistant.

Don't Play Shuffleboard, Break Through the Ceiling

Too many times when business leaders hear success stories of others who've found excellent Executive Assistants, they start playing shuffleboard–trying to fill the role with someone currently on their team. The more proficient the team member, the more likely they are to be in the running for the position. But if you have folks who are effective in their current roles, why would you risk undercutting their productivity by forcing them to play a position they weren't meant to play? That would be the equivalent of asking the best quarterbacks of all time to be the punter until they could find a replacement—ludicrous.

Steven's Team Reveals Their Struggle

As part of the intervention I mentioned earlier, a few members of my team revealed their frustration at being forced into the assistant role from time to time. I didn't intentionally undermine their productivity. I thought I was doing everyone a favor by saving money by not hiring myself an Executive Assistant. But when they said, "Hey, we love you, but we don't want to be your assistant. That's not my Unique Ability, and I didn't take this job to fill in like that," I realized I was robbing the entire team by trying to cut corners and pick the lock.

Others who value the players on their team may find themselves hiring support personnel for their high producers and neglect themselves. Maybe you're someone who has learned to value the extra production when your team is supported. At the same time, you're looking at the budget, and since you haven't dropped any of the balls you're juggling yet, you put off hiring your assistant. Your business is growing thanks to your team, but you haven't broken through the ceiling that will allow you to work to your highest potential.

It's interesting that your potential has a cap when you aren't supported. Most business leaders are aware of the pain involved as they struggle to keep the seesaw moving. Few understand the ceiling they create. It's hard to grasp the opportunity cost because it shows up in less intuitive ways—in frustration, failure, and friction. While other entrepreneurs are living the "sky is the limit" dream, those living under the pressure of the cap feel squished. They just can't break through. If that describes your situation, you might need to go back and sort out your self-limiting beliefs or find a coach who can help you shift your mindset and break the barrier.

Turning Over the Reins

After spending so much time leading a company, sometimes it's difficult for the entrepreneur to learn how to be managed. You are still the boss. It's still your company. However, a big part of finding success with an Executive Assistant lies in you and your team recognizing who is in charge. The shift in mindset will take time, and you have to set the example.

By the time most entrepreneurs add an EA, their team has grown accustomed to checking in with them on many levels. Some of these questions and check-ins will now belong to your Executive Assistant. It will take some training, but when you embrace the new reality, the rest of the company will as well. They may even be glad for the shift because answers will turn over more quickly. You won't be the block anymore. Eventually, even clients will start to turn to your assistant.

If you hoard tasks, you'll never learn to build trust in your assistant. Letting an assistant drive the relationship can be just as difficult as riding in a car with your teen just after she gets her license. We like being in control, but hoarding tasks outside your Unique Ability will make this investment in an assistant a waste of time and money.

After you put the right Who in place, a few questions will help you shift your mindset.

- Who is the more organized—you or your assistant?
- Who is more detail-oriented?
- Who best understands where you want to be and sees all the demands put on you?

Your assistant is in the best position to lead because she is keeping track of your life. She has a better perspective. The entrepreneur is too close to every aspect of the company and sometimes too emotionally involved to truly see the big picture. It's difficult to read the label when you're inside the jar.

Even if you enjoy organizing and exploring the details, you have only so much mental energy. You need to save it for your unique abilities. How can you make the most value and biggest impact on the world? Entrepreneurs tend to get distracted. and they often feel disoriented by the roller coaster ride of ideas and conversations they experience every day. We all need someone to bring us back to center. It's important to allow your assistant to drive the relationship.

Avoid Hustle Porn

Many entrepreneurs have lived in a state of constant motion for so long that they don't know what to do with their Free Days. Some call it being a workaholic, while others believe it's the only road to success. Either way, it's easy for us to get addicted to the hustle.

Hustling isn't a bad thing. We're entrepreneurs; keeping still isn't part of our nature. But when the hustle controls us instead of the other way around, it becomes a problem. We've all seen dogs who walk their owner. The way the animal drags the human down the street is comical, but it's no way to live your life. It's important to develop disciplined habits to avoid the pitfalls of distraction and lost productivity.

Unfortunately, just because we look busy doesn't mean we're being productive. We hop on social media to do some marketing. Ninety minutes later, we realize we dropped down a rabbit hole and need to climb back out.

Sadly, the effects of hustle porn can be just as deadly as drug and alcohol addictions. From mental health trauma and shortened lifespan to ruined relationships, trying to pick the lock to success by keeping busy instead of being productive is tremendously destructive. Numerous reports and surveys have been conducted to give us insight into this danger:

- A New York Enterprise Report survey noted that small business owners work twice as much as regular employees, with 33% working more than 50 hours per week and 25% working more than 60 hours a week.
- 72% of entrepreneurs are directly or indirectly affected by mental health issues compared to just 48% of non-entrepreneurs. (NIMH)
- 49% of entrepreneurs deal with mental health issues, while only 32% of their counterparts experience them. (NIMH)
- 45% of entrepreneurs report being stressed compared to 42% of "other workers." (Gallup Wellbeing Index)
- Entrepreneurs are more likely to have "worried a lot"
- 34% vs. 30%. (Gallup Wellbeing Index)

In addition, entrepreneurs were found to be more likely to experience the following in comparison to the general population:

- Depression: 30% compared to 15% (APA)
- ADHD: 29% compared to 5% (NIMH)
- Addiction: 12% compared to 4% (SAMHSA)
- Bipolar diagnosis: 11% compared to 1% (NIMH)

Entrepreneurs must stop glorifying the seventy-hour work week and the sacrifices we make in our relationships and health. We have to beware of getting caught up in the highlight reels of social media entrepreneurial life—a false representation that drives a fear of missing out. We must abandon the idea that our lives are in competition with others.

Instead, it's time to define victory on your own terms. Success is not a one-size-fits-all formula. Your path and priorities will not look like anyone else's. Take David's story, for example:

> *As an entrepreneur with multiple hats, life can get a little turbulent and bumpy. Slowing down is rarely a desirable option because I have places to go. Having an EA as a copilot upgrades the ride from a crazy bush pilot experience to a much smoother flight. I can focus on navigating to all these faraway destinations while Pia handles all the minute tasks and details. And that's a superpower!" —David Salerno, Entrepreneur Sherpa Co.*

An Executive Assistant gives us the edge in avoiding hustle porn. She helps us optimize our time and focus on our own definition of accomplishment. With an EA in the lead, we have fewer meetings, more focused tasks, and less distraction. The Executive Assistant knows when we need a lunch meeting with another entrepreneur whose vision and goals are similar to ours. Surrounding yourself with these like-minded individuals who prioritize balance and well-being rather than status and wealth can be a huge boost to developing disciplined habits.

There is something to be said about enjoying the journey. Adventure defines entrepreneurial life. We need to take time to soak in the experience and celebrate the small wins and milestones along the way. By putting an EA in the lead, you'll have help avoiding the burnout and setbacks that accompany hustle porn.

Balancing the Roles of Entrepreneur and Parent

Female business leaders have a few hurdles to jump that other entrepreneurs might not face. Some fall into the category of self-limiting beliefs, and others are just facts of life that we need to address. And while women let these questions and concerns limit them more often than men, many fathers find themselves looking for the key to escape the guilt as well.

Mom, We need shoes! But we don't need you to make them for us!
We love you,
The Cobbler's Kids

Mothers especially avoid hiring an Executive Assistant due to the fact that the moment their children are born—and sometimes before—they feel a need to take care of everyone and everything. Their nurturing instinct kicks in, and it carries over to the office where they support everyone but themselves.

Primary caregivers often put a ceiling on their career, assuming they can't climb too high until they finish raising their children. Most working mothers spend about twenty-one hours each week on household duties in addition to their professional duties. [2] Even with a nanny in place, they worry they can't be the parent they want to be if they focus on their Unique Ability or grow their business.

An Executive Assistant can be the pivotal piece in balancing work and home. Because you can be free to take time off to spend with the kids and have confidence the business won't implode without you, you never have to miss important moments in your children's lives. The EA knows your kids and helps you plan quality outings and special days.

But even more than that, you aren't working until midnight six days a week. You don't just show up for their events; you show up happy and without stress. If you feel exhausted when you finally slow down to spend time with your family, or you feel as though they only get the dregs of you—mom or dad—you need an Executive Assistant.

Destressed Shannon

My kids are college-aged now, but I still remember the exhaustion I felt before Nicole came on my team. I wanted to be calm at home and show them my best self, but even when I was home, I wasn't always present because I knew I'd be working as soon as they went to bed. I shorted myself on sleep to get everything in the house, and the workday done and ended up going to the office with a headache about half the time.

Yes, I had a nanny, but it was still ridiculous. Not having the support of a Strategic Assistant impacted my family in more ways than I can explain. I don't want any parent to go one more day without this resource so they can bring their best selves for their kids and spouse too.

Meet Steven's Wife

My wife, Corey, is my best friend and an awesome mother. In addition to her professional life, we have three children, two horses, two dogs, three miniature donkeys, and a mule named Michael Bolton. She's my business partner, working as the Integrator[3] for our boutique vineyard and live music event center, BarnHill.

She really makes everything look easy. I liken her to a duck gliding along the surface of a lake, looking elegant and leisurely while paddling furiously under the surface. However, when I began to list everything she was responsible for, I knew she needed help.

When I suggested she hire an Executive Assistant, she hedged. Self-limiting beliefs held her back. She said things like "I'm good," "It will be more hassle than it's worth," "We don't need to spend money on it," "I don't have enough to keep her busy," "I will have to pass off things I like," and "I don't want someone in my personal business."

Eventually, Corey agreed, and we brought Diana into our business to manage Corey. The results were transformational. Diana took on many of Corey's tasks and freed her to work on the parts of the business she loved most and focus on our children rather than the operations of our household. She became energized and better able to fulfill her most significant priorities. Corey is proof you can be a present parent and a successful business leader and love doing both.

It's time to change the mindset that coordinating every detail of family life is essential to loving your children well.

Trading true presence for busyness simply leads to stress, guilt, and feeling completely unfulfilled.

Takeaways

1. One major pre-qualification for hiring an Executive Assistant is the business leader's willingness to relinquish control of his or her calendar and inbox.
2. Delegating down implies you're passing off work to someone who can't handle more than the one task given to them. Shift your mindset to think of turning over these tasks as delegating up. Reframe the jobs you give your assistant as meaningful instead of menial.
3. People with the personality for the Executive Assistant position thrive on organizing. They see the thousands of emails in your inbox as a challenge, not the most dreadful part of their job.
4. No task is too small—every tiny thing you do is vital to the success of the company.
5. With an EA in the lead, we have fewer meetings, more focused tasks, and less distraction. Save your mental abilities for engaging in your unique abilities.

It's a Crock Pot, Not a Microwave

If you take a sincere interest in others,
they'll take a real interest in you.
Build relationships, don't collect them.

—Rebekah Radice

We live in a microwave world. Our great-grandparents thought nothing of waiting for a postcard from their friend on vacation. Today, we share our roller coaster rides live on Facebook and YouTube. Business documents, once delivered by the postal service or couriers, now come within seconds by email, and with the advancements in AI, our expectations rise daily. We get frustrated when webpages take more than nanoseconds to load, and heaven forbid your friend takes more than a few minutes to reply to your text.

Unfortunately, this same mentality can flow over into what you expect of your relationships. But relationships are forged in a crock pot, not a microwave. It takes time to build real trust and learn how to communicate. And while you can intentionally turn the heat up on the relationship to create space to get to know the other person better—much like you can a crock pot—you cannot simply rush through steps to get to the other side.

It's much like Warren Buffet's philosophy on compounding interest. If you really want to make money, you invest and then allow it to work through the downtrends as well as the ups. According to Buffet, every time you give up on an investment and move to another simply because it's not going well at the moment, you lose money.

The same is true with relationships, and perhaps none more than the entrepreneur-Executive Assistant relationship. Building the bond that can bring you the highest level of freedom and growth takes time, energy, and patience. You'll have days that feel like nothing goes right. Isn't that how life rolls? We can't give up. Otherwise, we'll miss out on huge returns on our investment.

Shift Your Mindset

That's one of the major mindset shifts entrepreneurs and business leaders must make when they begin exploring the idea of adding an Executive Assistant—this person is an investment in your business and in you. It looks costly; however, every person we know who has peaked on the Superpowered Scale has transitioned their thinking to see the compounding interest in this investment rather than focus on the cost.

Each of us has come to the realization we cannot afford NOT to have our assistants. They have become vital to our businesses, our families, and our personal health and well-being. Resisting this transformation in mindset holds back more business leaders than any other thing we've encountered in coaching entrepreneurs and helping them make the breakthrough to a 10X impact.

More Valuable than Anyone Ever Imagined—Steven Neuner

As my insurance business grew, a private equity-backed company offered to buy me out. Before we signed the deal, they generously gave me the opportunity to cut any unnecessary expenses so I could maximize the purchase price. They especially wanted me to understand the cost involved with having my assistant. They thought they were helping me see a bigger future.

I would be lying if I told you I didn't even bother doing the math. Her salary, including taxes, insurance, and benefits, had a half-million-dollar impact. Their down payment already meant a substantial financial life change for our family, and it could have been five hundred thousand more. However, I easily declined. I had united with them to help accelerate a much larger vision for our team and agreed to a two-year earnout with a performance-based payout if we grew the revenue of the company. I knew I didn't want to do that without my assistant.

The buyout company was stunned when I told them I would be keeping my assistant. (And they may have second-guessed their investment in me.) However, we achieved something largely unheard of in a very short

---

time. We reached the maximum increase in one year while I took one hundred fifty-five free days with my family. Additionally, we created massive value for the new organization, resulting in me getting the max earnout—five times my investment in my Executive Assistant. It also resulted in giving me additional performance grants so I could provide ongoing leadership after the earnout was complete.

We reaped the rewards of a compound interest investment. Our teamwork, combined with me being able to spend years in my Unique Ability, set the entire company free. My Executive Assistant allowed me to not only grow the business but also build and pour myself into a championship team of amazing leaders who each took ownership of the vision and gave me room to focus on what I did best.

We've given you some truly awesome examples of the benefits of hiring an Executive Assistant; however, the big results didn't happen overnight. Seeing the return on hiring an Executive Assistant won't take as long to see as the increase in your investment portfolio. At the same time, you can't look at this relationship like microwave popcorn.

We call the process Crawl, Walk, Run[IP]. It's a way to pace your expectations. By stopping to evaluate every thirty days, you can course-correct more easily and avoid some of the pitfalls that come with microwave relationships.

Learning to Crawl

Relationships are forged in a
Crock Pot, Not a Microwave.
—Steven Neuner

As soon as you make the brave decision to hire an Executive Assistant, it's time to create a list of everything you do in a two-week period—regardless of how small you think the activity might be.

My Two-week Activity Log

	Activity	Unique Ability?
1		
2		
3		
4		
5		
6		
7		
8		
9		
10		
11		
12		
13		
14		

Next, flag the activities that don't promote the best use of your time. At Superpowers, we divide these tasks into several categories:

- **Tiny:** Little tasks add up to big chunks of time. You should ideally be focused on what you love doing and are so good at that nobody else could replace you.
- **Tedious:** Not a great use of your time, and easy pickings for their Superpowers Assistant
- **Time-consuming:** More often than not, these are important but not urgent. A great opportunity for the 80/20 rule (80% of your results come from 20% of your efforts—so focus on that 20%)
- **Teachable:** It might cost you an afternoon, but are there tasks you should teach someone else on the team to handle? If so, the time to teach this task is an investment worth making
- **Terrible at:** It's not bad to admit areas you're weak in. Use language like "draining," "find frustrating," or "keep putting off" rather than "Hey, I'm useless at _____"
- **Time-sensitive:** Does your schedule get sliced and diced? A missed deadline because of limited availability isn't a good look for anyone, so let's take the time-sensitive ones off your plate
- **Tasks you love:** These are the energizing, constantly improving, nobody else on the face of this planet could do tasks. This is where you should be focusing 80% of your time

Every task in any of the first six categories should be delegated up to an individual with the unique abilities to handle them.

While going through the hiring process, you might consider recording yourself as you complete the tasks you'll be handing over to your EA—at this point, you have to do them anyway. You'll save yourself valuable time after your Executive Assistant begins because she can use the recordings to walk her through your processes and systems. She can pause where necessary, speed through what she already knows, and repeat them when a multi-step process requires an extra tutorial. You might even consider having her write the step-by-step process so you can review it and make sure she didn't miss anything. And when it's done, you have a valuable asset to add to training material for future hires.

During the first thirty days, your Executive Assistant will focus on you. We all have quirks and idiosyncrasies, things we like better than others, and specific ways we like information delivered. Learning those details allows your EA to put her Unique Ability into full function. By learning how much time you need to prepare for a meeting or the amount of information you need to feel ready for a presentation, your EA can optimize your calendar and set you up for success. Wouldn't you love finding all the notes, presentations, links, and names you need for your meeting right there in the calendar event?

This month will allow your new assistant to become fully aware of your business and personal goals—even the Big Hairy Audacious Goals. The more she learns and the sooner you let her in, the faster she will progress to give you a noticeable advantage as you become more productive and better equipped to handle each day. You might consider allowing your assistant to shadow you for a few days when they start—even if it's over Zoom. This will allow her to see how your day-to-day progresses.

During this initial period, we recommend a daily check-in—just five minutes. It could be a Zoom meeting or a phone call on the way home from the gym. This gives business leaders a minute to share what's on their mind and get a run-through of what the schedule looks like for the next twenty-four-hour period. Assistants also have an opportunity to tell the entrepreneurs how they can prepare to take on the day strategically and ask non-urgent questions so they can understand their entrepreneurs and their habits better. The best part of this meeting is that the key leader isn't responsible for organizing or setting up this engagement. The EA takes the lead and creates an agenda that not only keeps both the EA and the entrepreneur on task, but it also helps build the relationship.

Another important aspect of this meeting is the opportunity to give and receive feedback. Too often, busyness and fear of disrupting the relationship will create a desire to "batch" deliver problems. This means a series of insignificant tweaks become a tsunami of negativity. Unfortunately, the delivery is usually stress-driven, so it ends up being received in the worst possible light. The daily check-in also helps the entrepreneur avoid long meetings that have the potential to focus on problems. Many business owners will find reasons not to meet when this happens, creating bottlenecks and leading to a breakdown in the relationship. Don't wait until the last straw; deal with each unpleasantness as it comes.

Shannon Had to Learn How to Let Someone Else Lead

Nicole was my first Executive Assistant, and though she's moved on to explore a new entrepreneurial passion, we're still good friends. In fact, she's the one who coached me on how to be a good person for whom to work - something for which I'm deeply grateful. One of the things I enjoyed most about our relationship was the beautiful way she taught me about communication and the importance of handling points of friction and misunderstandings as they came up. We started our relationship using *The Communication Builder*® tool I created for the Strategic Coach Team Programs, and it became a critical part of our success. This tool is available on SuperpoweredBook.com

Daily huddles proved to be a huge asset to our relationship—a resource I still use with Katrina. Early in our partnership, Nicole asked, "Does anyone sit down with you and make a plan for what's happening ahead?" When I answered in the negative, she immediately scheduled a meeting with me in a nearby café.

I'm accustomed to leading meetings, but as I started to do that in this first Strategic Planning Meeting, she said, "Just hang on a second; I have an agenda." She came prepared and took charge. That was the most amazing experience for me. I sat back and let her lead, and that meeting set the tone for the rest of our relationship. I loved feeling supported. It was such a big relief to not have to be in charge for a change.

Another great way to get your assistant quickly acclimated to how you like things done is to invite her to organize for you. Call on her to find the appropriate project management system, something like Asana or Trello, and give her permission to either complete the organization process for you or tag team with you so you're both using your unique abilities to their fullest. This simple shift allows the Executive Assistant to learn your workflow process and schedule time in your calendar to take care of any part of the project only you can do.

Some entrepreneurs and assistants truly dive into this idea of relationship building. Others go into this hard with a "let's get this work done" attitude. It's vital to find a balance between the two. You don't want to sacrifice the relationship for productivity. At the same time, the key to multiplied productivity is a strong relationship.

These first thirty days will give your EA an opportunity to watch for when you're most productive so she can make sure your schedule leaves room for you to excel. This "getting to know you" period lets your assistant become familiar with your routine and witness your strengths and weaknesses.

The most difficult thing the entrepreneur will learn to do during these four weeks is to give the assistant room to lead. The EA will initiate regular meetings with the business leader and build a communication cadence that works for both the assistant and the entrepreneur. He or she will learn when to reschedule meetings and which projects need to be pulled forward.

> **Entrepreneurs and key leaders need to be fed and watered regularly.**
> —Shannon Waller

By the end of the month, your assistant will have learned how to read you. She'll know when to send you to the gym or give you a snack so you can get back into flow. She may discover you need water and snack breaks built into your schedule to keep you at optimal performance.

It's important to assess how the relationship is progressing at the end of the Crawl stage. It will be tempting for business leaders to measure tasks based on their last interaction with the EA rather than the entire experience. And while task-based feedback is tremendous, the most productive assessment will zoom out to evaluate the entire relationship. At Superpowers, we measure using a plus/

plus-minus/minus scale. While plus doesn't mean perfection on any level, it tells us you feel confident in your assistant's ability in that area. Plus-minus tells everyone we're not there yet, but with a little guidance, you see potential. And minus indicates a need for targeted effort for growth for both the EA and the entrepreneur. For example: Does the assistant take the lead in the relationship most of the time? Are your communication styles and cadences compatible? Have you begun to build trust? Has the entrepreneur started to leave his or her inbox alone? No one is perfect, but this scale allows you to judge which aspects of the relationship need the most attention.

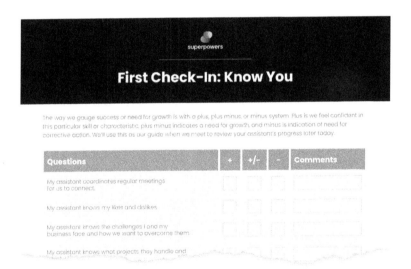

As important as it is for the EA to learn about you, you need to take these thirty days to get to know your assistant. Where has she worked before? What, besides organizing, does she love to do? Does she have children? What does her husband do?

Ryan's Confession

I thought I knew my first EA, but years into our relationship, I noticed she kept correcting our accountant's mistakes. I finally asked her about it and discovered she had worked in bookkeeping for many years. I started to wonder how much of her Unique Ability I was missing out on because I had only explored the surface of our relationship.

One of the biggest wins during the crawl stage is the development of trust. We need to think of trust like a bank rather than a vase. We've all heard the phrase, "We build trust." And the sentiment is true. Trust develops gradually. Instead of looking at this relationship like a vase or a jar—something you fill and only grows as we feed it—we need to begin to see it more like a bank that pays compounding interest. Every trustworthy thing a person does is a deposit, and every mistake takes a small withdrawal from the account. But since trust compounds with every success, a failure barely touches it.

On the other hand, each deposit also allows the other person to make a small withdrawal. We do this when we trust the other person with information about ourselves or tasks we're a bit protective of. After a number of deposits, the trust compounds to the point we can make large withdrawals because it's grown into unlimited trust in the person we're working with.

Trust goes both ways and will be the hinge pin that allows this relationship to reach its maximum potential. We understand the hurdles that stand in the way of earning and giving trust; however, entrepreneurs and Executive Assistants who focus on this aspect by sharing honestly and kindly and being open and transparent will have the best chance of success.

At the end of the first thirty days, you should feel as though the Executive Assistant has begun to know you well and vice versa. She knows your routines and preferences as well as the names of your family and closest friends. Your EA will start to recognize your personal strengths and weaknesses, and the drop in stress should begin to be noticeable. But this is just the first phase of the relationship.

These are just a sample of the evaluation statement and questions Superpowers uses at the end of the first month:

- My assistant coordinates regular meetings for us to connect.
- My assistant knows my routine.
- My assistant helps reduce my overall stress level.

Beginning to Walk

As you move into the second phase of building the relationship, honesty and transparency become imperative. While few go into this partnership thinking, *"I'm going to hide things and be dishonest,"* we don't always consider the importance of taking the time to share how we feel about things. This means sometimes we'll delve into the uncomfortable as we invite each other into our lives.

At the same time, you'll both begin to have more confidence in your communication level. In fact, you may develop your own language by this time. In-depth explanations will start to fade into keywords and phrases that both the entrepreneur and EA understand.

The thirty-to-sixty-day period can prove to be the most dangerous if you don't know what to watch for. After spending years overworked and overwhelmed, entrepreneurs can be tempted to delegate too much too early. Watching someone use their gifts to quickly move through tasks that once held you hostage creates a level of confidence that can lead to complications because the EA needs time to work through the process.

Working with Superpowers was like finding a hidden 3x lever on my productivity. And because of the program, the lever gets longer over time.
–Chris Facey, TForce Worldwide

Seeing how good they have it after thirty days has the potential to breed impatience in the entrepreneur. Your EA knows you well, and you're ready for her to anticipate your every move; however, each stage has a purpose. The Walk Stage gives your Executive Assistant time to *understand* you.

Another danger lurks beneath the waters in this leg of the relationship. The relief you feel when you start having true Free Days and no longer have to wade through endless emails can actually hamper communication. It becomes easier to settle for good enough rather than being honest about how we'd like to see things done—whether you're the boss or the leader. Business leaders sometimes feel pressure to hold back honest feedback for fear of losing what feels like lifesaving oxygen. Polite dishonesty is not the answer. The relationship needs you to keep it kind and keep it flowing when it comes to communication. It's the only way you'll reach your maximum potential. Constructive feedback goes a long way toward improving productivity, strengthening the partnership, and transitioning "good enough" into great.

At Superpowers, we train EAs to encourage feedback and suggest these strategies:

1. Frame feedback from a growth mindset.

2. Create regular feedback opportunities, so they become expected.
3. Use the plus, plus-minus, minus scorecard

At the end of your second month together, your Executive Assistant will understand which projects drain or energize you because she'll have seen which tasks constitute the best and worst uses of your time. By the end of sixty days, you may think it can't get any better, but if you're doing it right, the best is yet to come.

Here are a few of the evaluation statements Superpowers uses to overview the second thirty days:

- My assistant understands which activities are and are not the best use of my time.
- My assistant proactively takes things off my plate and handles them well.
- I have confidence my assistant will help me achieve new levels of freedom and growth in the future.

Free to Run

As you move into month three—assuming you've had intentional conversations, transparent sharing, and given your EA room to lead—your Executive Assistant now *Knows You* and *Understands You*. During this next thirty days, she will begin to *Anticipate* you.

For sixty days, she has listened to you make decisions and watched you handle tough situations. You've shared so intentionally that she understands why you made specific choices. Communication in the first sixty days plays a vital part in reaching Stage Three. It's vital to bring your assistant in on every decision, to describe your reasoning and the factors you considered. If you've worked hard to get through the first two stages and truly shared your mind, in this phase, you'll start to see your Executive Assistant get ahead of you—you'll feel as though she can read your mind.

Shannon Shares One of the Strengths of Strategic Coach

One of the things that makes the Strategic Coach office such a great place to work is the fact that Dan Sullivan is a great communicator. One of his massive strengths is being aware that his team needs the why behind any project. He's always setting the context by telling us things like, "Here's why I changed that," or "Let me explain my thinking in this." When you share the "Why," people can get on the same page with you.

Your inbox will be clear of anything you don't need to deal with, and your calendar will have blocks of time set aside for self-care. Uber Eats might begin showing up at your doorstep from time to time, or a Free Day you didn't know you needed will appear in your schedule. You'll find regular check-ups with your dentist and doctor begin to pop up out of nowhere—you didn't explicitly ask for these appointments, but your EA knew you needed them.

Because she knows your tastes and nature, your Executive Assistant will suggest concerts and shows coming to town. And if you've let her into your family life, you'll hear about ideas for Free Days with your kids at least a few times a year—events you would have completely missed because you don't have time to research fun family outings. Superpowers has created the *Better Partner and Parent Playbook* to empower this part of the entrepreneur-assistant relationship. But even without this tool, when your Executive Assistant is given free rein to work in her Unique Ability, her servant heart will emerge, bringing joy to your life outside of the work context.

With time, your EA will learn how to build your calendar around your energy. She will understand which tasks you perform better first thing in the morning and which ones require a break after they are completed. You'll feel as though she can read your mind.

Here are a few of the evaluation statements Superpowers uses at the end of ninety days:

- My assistant optimizes my schedule for my mental and creative energy.
- My assistant anticipates projects and handles them effectively.
- My assistant helps reduce my overall stress.

Not Effortless But Fun

At the end of the first quarter, the fun begins. The relationship isn't done growing. In fact, it will continue to evolve as long as you and your EA both stay growth-minded. You each are changing and discovering new things about yourselves, so the relationship will have to change

> I don't want people to 10X just their business. I want them to 10X their lives.
> —Steven Neuner

with it. Nevertheless, because everything seems to move so fast and you feel tremendously productive, the work becomes fun. Yes, it still takes some effort, but there's so much more joy in the journey; the work becomes almost like play!

Takeaways

1. Relationships are forged in a slow cooker, not a microwave. It takes time to build real trust and learn to communicate. Building the bond that can bring you the highest level of freedom and growth takes time, energy, and patience.
2. An EA is an investment in your business and in you. To peak on the Superpowered Scale, you have to transition your thinking to see the compounding interest in investing in your EA rather than focusing on the cost.
3. Crawl, Walk, Run. By stopping to evaluate every thirty days, you can course-correct more easily and avoid some of the pitfalls that come with microwave relationships.
4. Have your EA focus on you during the first thirty days. This month will allow your new assistant to become fully aware of your business and personal goals. This "getting to know you" period lets your assistant become familiar with your routine and witness your strengths and weaknesses.
5. After going through the Crawl, Walk, Run process, you will continue to evolve as long as you and your EA both stay growth-minded. But because everything seems to move so fast and you feel tremendously productive, the work becomes fun.

Nine Habits of the Ultra-High Performer

You make up the rules to your own game.
Design them so you can win.

—Dan Sullivan

Throughout the years, we've discovered that the highest entrepreneurial performers share at least nine constructive habits. No one builds these overnight. Each one begins with small changes, which, by habit stacking, build into a powerful force.

Each of the following habits stems from a shift in thinking regarding an Executive Assistant and adding the right person to your team. With this powerful force in place,

it's time to start stacking habits to create the freedom and growth of your dreams.

Habit #1: Time Blocking

To boost productivity, create your ideal weekly schedule and share it with your Executive Assistant. You have a big vision and a tremendous Unique Ability. It's time to allow her to mold your calendar around your goals. If we want to grow and be truly free, we have to ask ourselves often, "How does today play into my tomorrow?"

We recommend creating a list of all your activities at least once a year to see how the growth of the last twelve months has molded you. What tasks have you picked up that need to be passed along to someone who can give them more attention? Which jobs have you always enjoyed but they no longer fit your freedom/growth agenda? By reviewing key points, your assistant can become even more strategic in planning your day-to-day.

> My assistant turns my procrastination into productivity. Now, Free Days are no longer "Guilt" days. They are truly free!
> —Steven Neuner

While it seems obvious, many entrepreneurs need to be reminded to review and communicate their ideal week with their Executive Assistants at least quarterly. Your assistant cannot be a Strategic Partner if she doesn't know what your goals and strategies look like. At Strategic Coach, we have The Entrepreneurial Time System®, which is made up of Free Days, Focus Days, Buffer Days®.

Free Days are exactly that–free. You don't check email or answer work texts. You set aside an entire twenty-four-hour period, midnight to midnight, concentrating on the person you are outside your business. The purpose of Free Days is to rejuvenate yourself–to recharge your batteries. This might be time you spend with your family or friends or enjoy a hobby you'd miss out on otherwise.

Focus Days give you time to intentionally focus on money-making activities, ideally those that are within your Unique Ability. And Buffer Days allow you to prepare for your Focus Days and Free Days. Strategic Coach puts a heavy emphasis on Free Days. We block them out before anything else gets on the calendar.

Shannon's Free Days

Even though we're only halfway through this year, I have all my Free Days for the next calendar year blocked off. If I don't, they'll quickly get filled up, and I know I need those days to bring my best to my Focus Days.

Being intentional about how many Free Days, Focus Days, and Buffer Days you want each month and making sure your EA knows how you want your quarter to go become crucial elements in time blocking. Everyone's calendar will be different based on goals and how you best use your mental energy. What your schedule looks like isn't important; having your time intentionally blocked is.

Habit #2: Let Your EA Manage Your Personal Life and Personal Projects

What do scheduling plumbers and finding the perfect date night have in common? They're both perfect opportunities for your EA to shine. We know you're perfectly capable of doing these things yourself, and we realize we've said something like this at least once in the book already, but this point is THAT imperative to your success.

This is another reason it's best not to make your Executive Assistant a shared resource. She won't have the bandwidth to save you the sixty-two hours a year you spend making phone calls about haircuts and scheduling repair people to take care of your house if she's helping multiple individuals.

> Come to find out, Valentine's Day is February 14th every single year. Thanks to my EA, it no longer sneaks up on me!
> —Steven Neuner

Your assistant wants to help you keep the main thing the main thing. She knows your goals are greater than simply what you plan to accomplish in the business. You might not think about it, but the goals you share with your EA should include staying married, being a good parent, and keeping your house in good working order.

It's vital that we break through the mental barrier that says, "This is a personal thing, and I have to take care of it." Who in the world created this rule? It's time to take ownership of your life and make your own rules, which means recognizing that for an entrepreneur, there is no distinction between work life and personal life. They intersect on every level, so why shouldn't your EA help you navigate on every level?

She knows how much sleep you need and when your optimal workout time is. Let your EA put these things on your calendar, and then listen to her—let her lead.

Additionally, if you've given your Executive Assistant a list of all the important dates in your life—birthdays and anniversaries of family and friends, as well as special occasions you want to create for the people you care about, she will prompt you to plan or hand her the reins to move forward on it. Some think this means you haven't worked as hard for the people you love. But let's face it, you have a lot on your plate. Without prompting, nothing will happen, regardless of your beautiful intentions. The purposeful act of inviting your EA to manage even these parts of your life is an act of caring.

> I can't imagine my life without having my Executive Assistant's support to make sure everything runs smoothly. She lays down the track ahead of me and picks up the pieces after me, allowing me to do what I do best in the moment. —Shannon Waller

Habit #3: Daily Syncs

We mentioned this earlier, but we don't want you to think this should only happen during the first ninety days. If you want a winning EA-Entrepreneur relationship, daily meetings are a must, even in year twenty.

From the beginning, this should be an Executive Assistant-led meeting. For most business leaders, that single statement brings tremendous relief. Entrepreneurs are seldom meeting-type people. They might thrive in a brainstorming session; however, preparing for and attending long, drawn-out update conversations drains their mental energy. This is a time for the EA to shine. Each daily sync will have a few things in common.

1. The meeting might start with something that looks like an icebreaker question like, "What was the best vacation you ever took? How did you get there? What was the best part?" These questions allow the

EA to build the relationship and grow to anticipate the entrepreneur's needs and favorites.

2. The daily sync is the place to lay out the day for the entrepreneur. The assistant will give a brief heads-up for meetings and scheduling so the entrepreneur can get his or her head in the game. Plus, you can go over task lists to get updates and prioritize to-dos. If delegation needs adjustment, this is your chance to make it happen.

3. Email updates can also happen quickly. Do you have drafts waiting for approval, urgent messages, or overdue emails?

4. The EA becomes your personal and professional CRM during these few minutes. She'll remind you of important birthdays and anniversaries coming up, get information regarding gifts you want to send, and map out time for you to create personal notes.

5. Both the EA and the entrepreneur can use this five-to-ten-minute meeting to batch their non-urgent questions. Early on, this section may take a bit longer as the Executive Assistant gets to know you and begins to understand you better.

6. The daily sync also becomes another deposit in your relationship bank. Just like the trust bank delivers compound interest over time, the daily sync will allow this relationship to flourish.

Daily sync is one of the things entrepreneur Bo Barron loves most.

I meet with Alice every morning. On Mondays she gives me a rundown of my next ten workdays, and the other four mornings each week, she lists out my agenda for the day. Plus, she holds me accountable. Every day, she asks me if I've gone to the gym. It's something I asked her to do. Then, at the end of the day, she sends me a text with all the things we accomplished that day. It's amazing. Just having her on the team helps the brokerage business run better and frees me up to do what only I can do. —Bo Barron, Barron Commercial Group

The daily sync helps you ensure that the relationship doesn't stagnate, feeds your assistant's growth mindset, and allows you to stay aligned in your growth as you and your assistant evolve.

Let this meeting become a foundation for the rest of your day. Don't allow it to become a dreaded rule. Use it to keep things from falling through the cracks and remind yourself that someone has your back.

Shannon and Katrina Use the Daily Sync to Start Their Day with Positivity

Katrina and I start every meeting, including the daily sync, with a Positive Focus- something we're happy about or a place in our lives we feel like we're winning. Sometimes, it's personal, sometimes it's professional, and it allows us insight into what's important to the other person. It also means we're always bringing our best selves to the conversation!

Habit #4: Prioritize Replying to Your Assistant

Everything your assistant does is in your best interest. When you put off that reply, you are probably becoming the bottleneck for your entire company. Since she's trained to batch non-urgent questions, anticipate your responses, and make decisions on your behalf, if she calls, texts, or sends an email, it's urgent.

One of the primary complaints we hear at Strategic Coach from assistants is when the entrepreneur allows other meetings or calls to take precedence over communication with them. The highest performers go one step further than simply prioritizing replying to their assistant; they proactively communicate with their assistant when the schedule changes or they have an idea they want added to the next daily sync agenda.

Don't let the type of communication bog you down. Who created the rule that says you have to reply within the same media the assistant used to ask the question? What's the easiest way for you to close the loop for her? Even a short response will help keep your EA productive.

And finally, if you hesitate with your response, ask yourself why. What is the underlying reason? Do you not know the answer? Do you feel like you need more information? Is this not urgent to you, and it needs to be punted to the daily sync? Does it need more discussion than a text or a Loom video can communicate? Even if you can't answer your EA's question, any response will give her direction and allow her to move forward. Your assistant wants to support you; however, she needs you to prioritize communicating with her.

Superpowers loves to empower EAs to understand how to handle entrepreneurs when they begin to avoid tasks. We help them see the difference between conscious and subconscious avoidance and encourage them to approach the problem with caring and sensitivity. Those daily syncs can become crucial to determining why you're procrastinating. It's also a great place for the EA to look for signs of burnout. To help you understand these avoidance behaviors, we invite you to visit our resource library at SuperpoweredBook.com

Habit #5: The Highest Performers Give Each Valuable Team Member Their Own Executive Assistant

Once you experience the benefits of having an Executive Assistant, you'll naturally want to find EAs for each of your highly-paid executives. When each member of your team is able to work as their highest and best self, they'll become exponentially more productive.

Steven's History with Adding an Extra EA

Back in my insurance days, we acquired another agency, and with it, we inherited one of the highest-producing agents in the industry. We were warned of his abrasiveness, and few in the company liked the guy.

It didn't take long to discover that most of the things the old firm asked him to do were completely contrary to his Unique Ability. He was great at sales and thinking on his feet, but getting details and filling in all the blanks just wasn't in his wheelhouse. So, we hired an Executive Assistant to work exclusively for him.

The operations team was ready to fire this agent despite his outstanding performance because he was so hard to work with. However, within a couple of months of having his own assistant, people in the office liked him a lot more. He doubled his already record-breaking productivity, and with the EA reminding him about the details, he started thanking people and surprising them with small gifts. Talk about a huge strategic win!

Habit #6: More Than Your Inbox, Calendar, and Task List

The highest-performing entrepreneurs don't limit their Executive Assistants. They invest the time and resources to create proactive partners—people who take on tasks even before they're asked. EAs make great project managers, and they help smooth every friction point in a business leader's life.

For instance, a one-page brief of each person you'll meet that day can be a tremendous asset. You no longer have to remember spouses' names, colleges, hobbies, or every detail of every project. The assistant can put together all that information so you have it at your fingertips to review just before your meeting.

We recommend the EA send a Daily Brief. This is a daily email newspaper written especially for you. It gives an overview of everything going on throughout your day. Kevin Cumbus is one of our entrepreneurs who has become dependent on his Daily Brief:

> *April always has a great attitude and energy on our calls. She's always prepared and very organized. She sends beginning-of-day texts and end-of-day emails, and I find myself becoming more and more reliant on them. I open her email first now so I know what's important and most critical. That's a level of dependence I have never enjoyed before. —Kevin Cumbus, TUSK Partners*

Similarly, the Daily Bullet comes through at the end of the day. This short summary of the last eight to ten hours gives you peace of mind and allows you to be totally present at home. You leave the workplace confident and unencumbered.

You also don't have to do all the hiring. Your assistant can find special talent for key projects. From advertising to interviewing, she can alleviate that burden. This creative asset who loves to make sure things get done can easily take over projects for you. You might have every step mapped out in your brain, but we tend to get easily distracted. So, relieve the friction by passing the task and your steps to your assistant.

Ryan's EA Allows Him to Be Present at Every Meeting

I love knowing I never have to worry about running over during a meeting. Rather than watching my phone to make sure lunch isn't running too long, I have the assurance that if I haven't checked in with my EA to let her know I'm moving from one meeting to the next, she's going to call me giving me the perfect excuse to wrap up and get going.

Most entrepreneurs have just a few very deep skills. Everything else causes stress and drudgery. Let your Executive Assistant handle everything outside of those deep skills, and if you need two assistants to take care of all the other details, you'll quickly see the value.

Habit #7: Let Your Assistant Control Your To-Do List

To-do lists can be very deceptive. Every line item takes up the same amount of space on the paper, but they don't all require the same amount of time. With the EA scheduling them appropriately, the entrepreneur can cross more off his or her list. Plus, knowing a to-do that seems important has a place on a schedule can alleviate stress for the business leader.

When your EA has control of your project and to-do list, you might even see things disappear. She'll handle the things that fall in her Unique Ability, and she'll know your team well enough to pass along a task that can be more efficiently accomplished by someone else. Your Executive Assistant can also advise you when it's time to start looking for a Who to accomplish a task. If something sits undone on the list for too long, either it's outside your Unique Ability, it's a low priority for you, or you haven't got the right person on your team to accomplish it.

If you allow them, your EA can be your task filter. They can proactively work to keep things off your to-do list.

Habit #8: Use Efficient Communication Strategies

Early in your relationship, you need to let your EA know how you communicate best. One resource that has proven vital to the Superpowers EA-Entrepreneur relationship is the Strategic Coach *Communication Builder* exercise. It can help you better understand how to share with your team, your family, and your EA.

We often assume everyone operates the same way we do; however, it's just not true. With technology at our fingertips, we have a vast array of messaging tools, and your Executive Assistant needs to know which ones reduce stress and close loops in your mind best. Which method are you connected to most often? What strategy works most effectively when she's sending an entire file for you to review?

Some people enjoy face-to-face conversations over email. Others would rather have a text message. And it's not unusual for people to have one preference for giving information and another for receiving it. Having this piece of wisdom can give you a tremendous advantage as you become a high-performing entrepreneur.

Timing plays a crucial role here as well. Do you appreciate notes for your meeting twenty-four hours in advance, in the morning before you start your day, or ten minutes before you go into the conference room? The *Communication Builder* can give you a head start as you forge this relationship.

Ryan's Early Struggles

Some of my early struggles with my first Executive Assistant fell in the realm of poor communication. I wanted to onboard my assistant and take the time to share our core values and mission and explain my vision for her role in the company. Unfortunately, I was running back-to-back meetings at the time. I came out just long enough to give her access to my inbox and rushed back in.

Ideally, I also wanted to provide "early and often" feedback to course correct and give her the formation training she needed. However, I was so busy and disorganized, I ended up "batching" all my criticisms and letting them roll out like a tsunami. This usually happened because I was stressed or upset.

Fortunately, I learned from my mistakes and techniques I've discovered through Strategic Coach. This has enabled me to build better relationships and avoid common communication pitfalls.

When it comes to communication, drive-by delegation won't do. You can't rattle off your brain's top-ten list at lightning speed and then complain that your EA can't keep up. You put stress on your EA when you force her to remember number four on your quick list. Recording your list is a great way to close that loop in your mind while lowering your EA's stress level.

Habit #9: Let Your Assistant Lead

Yes, we've said this several times, but it might be one of the most difficult aspects of the EA-Entrepreneur relationship for the business leader. Letting go of the reins and giving your EA room to steer will make this a winning relationship. No longer will you decide what gets done next. Your assistant will be pulling things forward and you'll be providing resources and removing roadblocks in the things she brings to your attention.

As you level up because of your assistant, be certain to keep her in the loop so she can continue to lead into a future that is unknown, uncertain, and undefined. Having a thoughtful conversation with your assistant after you attend conferences or training can enrich your assistant's role and give her the tools she needs to push you forward. You'll soon realize you don't have to have all the answers. Your assistant becomes your thinking partner. When you let her in on your thoughts and uncertainties, you'll discover you don't have to go it alone.

Steven's Day After

I don't have words to express the value I find in my Strategic Coach sessions. I get so many insights and ideas. My brain is moving at a thousand miles an hour. Celeena and I have a plan that has catapulted our productivity. She blocks off the morning after every Coach session so I can debrief her. We spend a significant amount of time going over my notes and downloading the information from my brain. This allows her to stay a step ahead of me and lets her lead effectively.

Dan Sullivan says, "Be in charge, not in control." He means you need to provide the electricity and be the energy source for your team, fueling them and casting a bigger vision. At the same time, your Executive Assistant takes control of your time, your activities, and your energy so you can accomplish the things only you can do.

Habits aren't easily built; however, repetitive action will create the muscle memory you need to become like the Ultra-High Performers and transform into one yourself.

Takeaways

1. Create a list of all your activities at least once a year to see how the growth of the last twelve months has molded you. By reviewing key points, your EA can become even more strategic in planning your day-to-day. Your assistant cannot be a Strategic Partner if he or she doesn't know what your goals and strategies look like.

2. Successful EA-Entrepreneur relationships require daily meetings led by your Executive Assistant. The daily sync helps ensure the relationship doesn't grow stagnant, and it feeds your assistant's growth mindset. This allows you to stay aligned in your growth as you and your assistant evolve.
3. The highest performers proactively communicate with their assistants. Even a short response will help keep your EA productive.
4. Invest time and resources to create proactive partners—EAs who take on tasks even before they're asked.
5. Let your EA lead. Your assistant becomes your thinking partner and can continue to effectively guide you toward a future that is unknown, uncertain, and undefined.

The Key To Not Losing Your Mind

My productivity immediately quadrupled
when I hired my first full-time entrepreneurial assistant.
This is no mean feat.

—Shannon Waller

We considered adding "The Secret to Not Losing Your Mind" to the subtitle of this book. You can't imagine the amount of mental energy you regain when you add an Executive Assistant to your team.

Think about it—how many times every day do you second-guess yourself? The uncertainty of trying to remember what you've done, what needs to be done, who you delegated to do what, and more causes endless open loops in our minds. *Did I follow up with . . .? Did I remember to tell . . .? Where do we stand on that project? What is my next client's wife's name? I know he's told me a dozen times.*

Ryan's Victory

You can't imagine the incredible amount of mental energy you're spending on stuff that is not your Unique Ability. I didn't realize how many follow-ups and project management items I was involved in. When you begin to see how much you're keeping track of that your assistant takes over, you'll be amazed.

For instance, I love that when I go on sales calls, my sales briefs are always in order. I know the details about the person I'm meeting because Leslie takes time to identify common points of connection with prospects, giving us quick camaraderie. She removes every bit of unnecessary uncertainty, saving me time and lowering my stress level. Plus, the meeting is on my schedule without much thought on my part, and any member of the team that needs to be there has been invited. Leslie is my certainty solve. I know going into my day that my priorities have been taken into consideration, the entire team is pulling in the same direction, and the beautiful cohesion tracks back to my assistant.

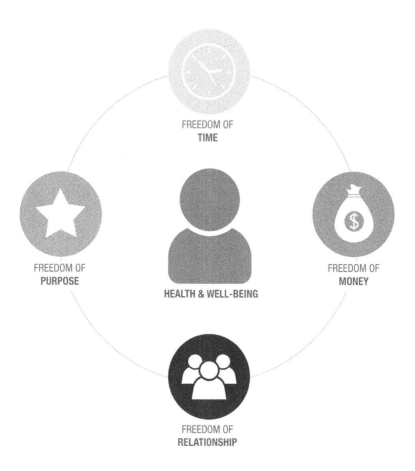

Every entrepreneur we've encountered has been amazed at the EA's ability to open the door to the Four Freedoms—freedoms that naturally produce growth. Not only did the entrepreneurs find more time and money, but they also experienced freedom in their relationships and freedom to live out their purpose, all in service of better health and well-being. The overwhelming results of hiring an Executive Assistant surpassed the entrepreneur's highest expectations.

Take Back Your Time

Prior to engaging an Executive Assistant, more than one entrepreneur complained about calendar management. Some found themselves double-booked on a few occasions. Others missed important moments in their children's lives. We hear things like, "I feel like I'm supposed to be in two or three places at one time." "I don't have time to prepare for meetings." "I can't ever take a day off." "I put in ten hours a day and don't accomplish anything." "I need two of me to be successful."

Their time is not their own.

When we introduce the idea of the business running like a well-oiled machine while the entrepreneur takes thirty consecutive days off, most business owners laugh. They think it might be possible for other companies but not theirs. Yet, within six months of hiring the right person, they begin to see light at the end of the tunnel.

Perhaps Bo's story will convince you:

Alice gives me back at least ten hours per week. Now, think about this. How valuable are those ten hours a week to me? I can look at it financially and say thousands of dollars. I can look at it socially and think about how I took my daughter golfing this week for the first time. I can look at it emotionally and consider my rest, well-being, and sanity. To me, she is invaluable. I'm creating more wealth because of her. I'm deepening my relationships with the people who matter most to me because of her. My mental health is better because of her. Having a great EA is an absolute no-brainer and a complete blessing. —Bo Barron, Barron Commercial Group

Having a skilled, trained professional with a passion for this career means you have a fully-managed calendar.

Your business agenda meshes with your personal life, and you begin to feel freedom from the stresses related to those statements we mentioned earlier. But even more, you find yourself with time to prepare for meetings—whether that means gathering information and creating a presentation or mentally organizing your thoughts so you can confidently fly by the seat of your pants. Additionally, the clock seems to slow as you focus on your passion. The project that took days morphs back into the six hours of fun just like when you started your company. An Executive Assistant not only gives you freedom from your calendar, but she also gives you freedom to enjoy every minute.

Don't Worry About Money

As we mentioned, many hold back on hiring an assistant because they don't want to splurge on themselves. Adding a line item to the budget makes them nervous. Yet, when you consider the time you get back with an Executive Assistant in the lead, you can easily translate that to dollars.

We've each found that the ability to become laser-focused on our unique abilities increases our production exponentially. We find bigger and more exciting opportunities to grow our businesses because the distractions of administration disappear. And, as we all know, productivity and bigger opportunities mean more income.

Consider what you would do with an extra five hours a week. Eric Rothman tells us he gained five hundred hours a year! How much extra revenue could you generate with an additional ten hours in your schedule each week?

Don't Sacrifice Relationships

Most entrepreneurs we meet struggle to balance home life with business. Single business owners don't see any hope of meeting someone to spend the rest of their lives with. They find it difficult to maintain business relationships, both internally and externally.

Even when entrepreneurs set aside an evening to spend with friends or family, their minds run back to the office or create tomorrow's to-do list. The pressure to grow their companies doesn't allow them to be present. We all remember missing milestones and precious moments with the people who matter most to us.

Not only does the Executive Assistant redeem the time necessary to cultivate and grow business and personal relationships, but she also actively participates in building the entrepreneur's most significant relationships. She knows the names of these important people and has a list of things they enjoy.

But it goes beyond that. The best Executive Assistants become invested in the entrepreneur they lead. These invaluable resources love being allowed to use their creativity to help you come up with unique ideas. An EA knows you and enough about your closest relationships to make suggestions—ideas you never would have come up with on your own. Because they care and see you as a whole person, the EA invested in your success won't stop with your work life. You can expect no more missed date nights, and you'll have the greatest potential to show up for every meeting functioning at your highest level. The merge of heart and mind within your EA gives you even more leverage to build strong relationships.

Steven Still Dates His Wife

I set the bar pretty high before my wife and I married. I've always had a creative entrepreneurial mind, so even before I realized that's what it was, I used it to plan awesome evenings. Every date was sort of an event. Unfortunately, running a business doesn't allow the extra time it takes to plan more than a meal at our favorite restaurant.

That's where my Executive Assistant stepped in. Fern started this years ago, and Celeena continues to help me be amazing. I gave them what I call my *Better Husband Playbook*. It's a list of all my wife's favorite foods, flowers, events, entertainers, and more. Each month, my assistant researches upcoming concerts, movies, and other fun stuff and gives me a list of what my wife and I could do for a special date night, including nearby restaurants. I pick the places, and my assistant takes care of the tickets, reservations, and my calendar.

After more than two decades, I still get to surprise my wife with extraordinary date nights while staying focused on my purpose and avoiding the distraction of multiple web pages and pop-up ads.

She also has a similar playbook for each of my children. If she sees something one of them would enjoy, she gives me a heads-up. Fern found a Cowgirl Museum and Rodeo I took my horse-enthusiast daughter to. I love being able to make awesome memories without losing hours lost in a web search.

When you choose to spend quality time with someone, your EA takes care of every detail. You get to be intentional in deciding who to spend time with and what you'll ultimately do, but your assistant makes the reservations, notifies everyone involved, and confirms the date or appointment. Plus, she manages you—so you arrive on time without anything on your mind other than strengthening the bond with the person on the other side of the table. Her advanced knowledge of your relationships allows you to show up as your best self.

This ability to actually grow relationships while you expand the business might be one of the most talked about benefits of adding an Executive Assistant to your team. More than one client has expressed the sentiments of Kevin:

> *As the CEO of a growing business, my time became my most important asset. I signed up for assistance with e-mail, scheduling, and travel planning. I gained a team member who knows me and my family and helps me be not just the best CEO I can be but the best husband, friend, and dad. April looks around corners for me and reminds me to schedule movies and golf outings with my son, date nights with my wife, and concerts with my daughter, all while keeping my business life in order. April has been a life changer for me, and I don't want to ever go back to life without an EA. Thank you, April, for all that you have done for me, my business, and my family!*
> *—Kevin Cumbus, TUSK Partners*

Renew Your Purpose

At the beginning of this book, Larry and Victor were encouraged to remember why they started their businesses. It's a question entrepreneurs need to return to often to keep them focused on their unique abilities and their purpose. What is your Why? How do you want to make an impact in your family or the world?

James A. Michener is credited with saying, "A master in the art of living draws no distinction between his work and his play; his labor and his leisure; his mind and his body; his education and his recreation. He hardly knows which is which. He simply pursues his vision of excellence through whatever he is doing and leaves others to determine whether he is working or playing. To himself, he always appears to be doing both."

The world is a better place when entrepreneurs are empowered to work in their Unique Ability and surrounded by a team who are all working in theirs.

The first thing to get lost in the tangle of administrative wires is the original vision that fueled the entrepreneur's passion in his or her initial years of building the company. Your business starts to feel a lot like work, and you don't have time to do the things that make it seem like play. Perhaps you felt a calling or were inspired to do something amazing. Maybe you started the business so you could fund something more missional. Unfortunately, without help, the chaos of balancing the spinning plates forces our focus away from our purpose.

With an Executive Assistant steering the boat, you can leave your post as navigator and return to being captain of your Unique Ability. She leads your team to take care of the routine tasks and the monster projects you aren't good at, freeing you to focus on the thing you were born to do.

Get Out of the Dark Gap

Too many entrepreneurs ignore their health. No one truly enjoys going to the doctor, so when it also interferes with the schedule, we make a greater effort to avoid those appointments. A daily walk or work-out feels like an extravagance to many business leaders. If you're already spending thirteen hours a day trying to get everything done and tucking your kids into bed is your longest conversation with them all day, adding an hour for the gym or making time to eat more than a few crackers for lunch seems impossible. Taking care of physical health concerns and creating healthy habits need to become a regular part of the entrepreneur's to-do list.

Steven's Healthy Habits

Thanks to my Executive Assistant, my calendar is blocked off intentionally to keep me healthy. I have gym time blocked off every day, and she even assigned a couple of days to the workouts that I hate. I hate leg day, but Celeena knows I am committed to it. So even though my legs look the same whether I lift every day or not, my calendar reminds me I need that workout a couple of times a week.

I used to work through lunch all the time, and snacks never happened. It's easy for me to get completely immersed in my work. But now, both my midday meal and my snack pop up in my reminders—as important as a meeting with a client.

Plus, I've gone to all kinds of doctor's appointments I never would have gone to without my assistant. I hate them, and I always put off that kind of stuff, but Celeena doesn't let me get away with that.

You might think skipping lunch every day is no big deal; however, research shows that in one thousand rulings, judges granted parole requests in sixty-five percent of cases at the beginning of their sessions and right after snack breaks and almost none later in the session. Some attribute it to mental fatigue, others to hunger. Either way, it demonstrates the effect taking care of our health can have on our decision-making. [4]

An even bigger problem is the struggle these startup gurus have with mental health. Surveys show that while some entrepreneurs work at their business twenty hours a week or less, fifty-eight percent work fifty or sixty hours. Sleep-deprived and feeling like a failure, it's easy to fall into the dark gap. Depression sets in, and feelings of helplessness overwhelm them. Nevertheless, too many keep the deep darkness to themselves, which compounds the dilemma. Even when these guys and gals do take a vacation, sixty-seven percent of them check in to work at least once a day.

According to the National Institute of Mental Health, seventy-two percent of entrepreneurs are directly or indirectly affected by mental health compared to forty-eight percent of non-entrepreneurs. Stress and worry eat them from the inside out. The thing that started out as their passion project begins robbing them of health and well-being—slowly killing them.[5]

Burned out and overextended, these small business owners feel anything but free. The entrepreneurial life is often viewed as glamorous; however, the mental toll makes it dark and dreary. And this element may be what makes the Executive Assistant most valuable.

Entrepreneurs tend to be like the Energizer Bunny™. They just keep going, using every ounce of mental energy they possess. An Executive Assistant with permission to truly manage the business leader can be a powerful force in keeping the entrepreneur from feeling like he or she is losing their mind. Christi learned this in the first few months of working with an Executive Assistant:

I seriously don't know how I would do this without my assistant. I mean, his attitude is fantastic. He constantly says, "I got it" "I'll take care of it." He is willing to take on whatever. For instance, I booked the wrong car service, and he fixed it for me while I was flying. He has taken so much stress and the "how in the world am I going to get all this done" off my plate. I truly don't know what I would do without him. —Christi Van Rite

The Executive Assistant finds ways to lighten the load of the entrepreneur and gives her boss a safe place to vent and time to recharge. The business leader has the mental and physical energy to pursue healthy habits and build better relationships. With the time and space to think creatively, entrepreneurs' talents naturally resurface, restoring health and allowing them to do what they love. Strategic Coach and Superpowers have excellent resources to help the Executive Assistant and business leader work together to alleviate the mental strain.

We see entrepreneurs make huge sacrifices when they get stuck in the Frustration or Delegation phases of the Superpowered Scale. Some sacrifice their marriage after years of no date nights. Others sacrifice finances because exhaustion skews their view of their business. No one should sell their company when they feel Resignation, Desperation, or Frustration. Entrepreneurs have sold out for millions less than their business' actual valuation because they didn't know their numbers, and their mental state blinded them to the truth.

Business leaders live in the land of compromise too often. They sacrifice time, money, relationships, purpose, and perhaps worst of all, health. There is so much more to owning a business than getting caught on the seesaw of success. It's time to truly be free!

Your Assistant's Assistant

Artificial Intelligence has moved into the forefront of technology. It's morphing so quickly it's impossible to predict what we'll be able to do tomorrow with its new capabilities. And change is often scary.

The bravest people admit to having a bit of fear associated with the digital assistants. Some lose confidence thinking the technology will replace them. Others don't trust it. But before we can take a deep dive, we need to understand what it is.

Think of AI as smarter automation. Evan Ryan and his team at *Teammate AI* describe it as computers doing tasks humans used to do or shouldn't do anymore. When we look at AI, we want to consider how the technology can save us time. How can it eliminate the things that bore us or the tasks we procrastinate on?

You may be thinking you can bypass an Executive Assistant if you engage AI, but we see it differently. We think of AI as your assistant's assistant[IP]. AI gives your EA incredible research capabilities by putting Perplexity.ai at her fingertips, as well as the powerful writing capabilities of ChatGPT and the creative image generation of DALL-E. A great Executive Assistant manages you so you can be free to work in your Unique Ability. AI is simply another tool to make your partnership more likely to succeed. It will allow your most valuable asset to do more stuff they do like and less stuff they don't. This tool can cut their research time and aid them as they book your travel and plan your next out-of-town adventure. With AI, your assistant can quickly summarize meetings, create lists of action items, and personalize repetitive emails.

You'll also need your Executive Assistant to clean up text that comes from any GPT. Even when given specific and unique prompts, GPTs will take your questions, combine them with information from the internet, and produce creative but not necessarily accurate copy. While you can invite AI to write your letter or craft a case study, you'll need a human element to double-check for relevancy, repetition, redundancy, and reality. Your EA has the critical content about your business, team, clients, and industry–specifics AI lacks. At the same time, AI can help her get up to speed on a new skill. It will also check facts, spelling, and grammar and even create presentation slides.

Superpowers offers several tools and playbooks to train Executive Assistants so they can get the most out of this growing technology. While your assistant frees you to work in your passion, AI and GPTs have the ability to give them the same flexibility so they can focus on what they do best.

To maximize the potential of your assistant, you'll want to provide as many tools as possible. Training like we offer at Superpower can be a start, and subscriptions to AI tools can be another. Fortunately, every penny you invest in your Executive Assistant is an investment in you.

Takeaways

1. The overwhelming results of hiring an EA allow you to find more time and money and experience freedom in your relationships, freedom to live out your purpose, and freedom to have better health and well-being.

2. Having a skilled, trained professional with a passion for this career means your business agenda meshes with your personal life, and you begin to feel freedom from the stresses.

3. The ability to become laser-focused on your unique abilities increases your production exponentially.
4. Don't sacrifice relationships. An EA reclaims the time necessary to cultivate and grow business and personal relationships and actively participates in building the entrepreneur's most significant relationships.
5. An EA can find ways to lighten your load, create a safe place to vent, and give you time to recharge. You will have the mental and physical energy to pursue healthy habits and build better relationships.

PART THREE

Superpowered

Confidence is the most important
capability an entrepreneur can develop.

—Dan Sullivan

Superpowered From the Executive Assistant's Point of View

The best part about being Superpowered is the fact that the transformation doesn't simply benefit the entrepreneurs and business leaders. We want every member of our teams to be able to thrive using their unique abilities, especially our Executive Assistants. In fact, we're hoping a few potential EAs will read this book and see themselves in the descriptions. To help you grasp the beauty of this career choice, we thought we'd let you hear from each of our tremendous EAs.

Celeena Leads and Manages Steven

I worked in the banking industry for almost a decade before I realized I was simply a robot moving pieces along on a conveyor belt. I felt as though I wasn't really making a difference, and the industry didn't treat its employees kindly. I needed a rebirth—a reset button. I wanted—no—I needed to make a difference. The endless, repetitive cycle felt pointless and inescapable.

Working in the back office of the bank gave me a taste of administrative work. Dealing with data entry, mail, invoices, and the like was awful. Someone would give me a stack of papers to organize or a list of emails to reply to. Nothing had any rhyme or reason. I knew I couldn't survive in that environment, though I didn't mind the tasks. But I needed to incorporate those skills into doing something with purpose. Researching the possibilities revealed a career as an Executive Assistant. I discovered Superpowers on an Indeed job posting and knew I'd found my match. I made it my life's goal to get hired!

I'm a very organized person with a futuristic mindset. As my mother likes to say, I tend to put the cart in front of the horse. But that mindset helps me avoid major surprises down the road. I foresee issues my entrepreneur might not think about, allowing me to intervene proactively and preventively. Knowing how to look around corners is a major Executive Assistant skill, and it's something I'm good at.

I've been using my Unique Ability to help Steven since 2022. Watching his life transition in a positive way and knowing my assistance as his EA has helped him get here is a huge motivator. Working together, we've seen him become more organized, freeing him to focus on the things he does best. More importantly, he has more time to spend with his family! I feel like my work gives him peace of mind and allows him to concentrate on keeping bigger projects moving forward.

> Steven: Please schedule that thing with that person; it's really important!
>
> My Executive Assistant: Already done!

Nothing compares to sharing in another's success and knowing that you helped create something magical, something with the potential to make someone else's life better, both personally and professionally. Being an Executive Assistant is so much more than processing tasks! I get to be a part of the decision-making process, provide feedback, and see a project through from start to finish. Watching others progress in their work and having hands-on access makes me feel like I'm part of the team rather than just an organizing pencil pusher.

We've accomplished so much since I started. Seeing him less stressed and looking forward to what we have coming up makes me feel like I've done my job well! This position has literally changed my life, and I have never looked back!

> *Dear Fern, Celeena, and All Amazing Executive Assistants,*
> *I am filled with gratitude and excitement as I write this letter to honor the incredible impact you have had on my journey as an entrepreneur and to extend my heartfelt thanks to all Executive Assistants who play such a crucial role in the success of entrepreneurs everywhere.*

Fern, you were my very first Executive Assistant, and together, we navigated the uncharted waters of my early entrepreneurial days. Your unwavering support, dedication, and loyalty laid the foundation for everything that followed. Though you've retired, the legacy of our partnership continues to inspire and guide me and so many others through the daily work of Superpowers every day.

Celeena, for the past two years, you have been a rock of support and enthusiasm. Your recent move from Pennsylvania to Texas to become our Operations Manager at BarnHill Vineyards is a testament to your incredible commitment and growth. With your husband joining us as the Vineyard Manager, we've added more all-stars to our team, and I couldn't be more thrilled for our next exciting chapter together!

Thanks to you both, the businesses we worked in together have been respected and admired. You have helped me choose the perfect gifts of appreciation for clients and team members, your warm first impressions have helped clients understand our commitment to service, not just sales. You've held me accountable, creating "collision courses" for difficult conversations I didn't want to have or important things I wanted to avoid. You supported me through tough decisions and helped me be present at key meetings even when I couldn't be there physically.

Beyond the professional realm, your support has been instrumental in maintaining a balanced and fulfilling personal life. Fern and Celeena, for my faith, you have protected my morning quiet time, championed "my passion" projects like Dogs on Heaven Street *and* Are You A Tree?, *and guided me through quitting points and moments of doubt. Your dedication has strengthened my 21-year marriage to*

Corey, ensuring we never missed a date night or an important milestone. You've played Tetris with my schedule to prioritize and even plan my family time, allowing me to be fully present on vacations and never miss an opportunity to drop my kids, pick my kids up from school, or attend a show or game. You made it possible for me to not just have moments but make moments special.

To all Executive Assistants, including my new assistant Regine, you are essential partners in our success. Every day, entrepreneurs take risks that others shy away from. We live entirely in the "Results Economy," where clients pay for outcomes, not the countless hours of effort behind the scenes. With the support of exceptional people like you, we can focus on where we create the most value while you execute essential responsibilities that keep everything running smoothly. This partnership not only amplifies our results but also keeps our energy high to tackle new challenges. Your dedication and unique skills make our achievements possible, and I am deeply grateful for all you do.

Fern and Celeena, thank you for everything. Our journey together has been nothing short of transformative, and I look forward to the continued growth and success we will achieve. Your contributions have unlocked potential, not just for me but for everyone we touch through our work.

With deepest gratitude,
Steven

Katrina Keeps Shannon on the Right Track

I started as a teacher, and I loved working with the children. Despite the meaningful and important work, I quickly learned I needed a job with just as much purpose but one that wouldn't hijack the rest of my life. I cared so deeply that I had become overwhelmed. The hours required outside the classroom eventually encompassed my entire life. Between the burnout and curriculum that didn't align with my values or teach young children the things I felt were deeply important, I knew I needed a career change.

I've always loved supporting people—personally and professionally. It comes quite naturally to me. I don't like the spotlight; I'm a much better fit for the backstage. So, after I called it quits on teaching, it seemed natural for me to look into supportive roles. In fact, nothing else ever crossed my mind. For as long as I can remember, I have loved being the planner, knowing all the details, giving good advice, and playing Tetris on expert level—my favorite game ever. These things come easy to me, and I enjoy them!

At first, I moved from teaching to the support staff for the legal and construction industries. The predictability of the work made them comfortable jobs, but they lacked significant challenges. Unfortunately, easy and comfortable can quickly become monotonous. So, every time I got near the two-year mark, I started feeling bored. And this feeling quickly spiraled into miserable tedium. I love predictability and stability, but I have a strong desire to grow and be challenged intellectually.

Being Shannon's Executive Assistant gives me the perfect blend of predictability laced with intellectual challenges. I also love that Strategic Coach is a growth-oriented business with a great company culture. I enjoy the profiles they invite us to do because it allows for better self-awareness, and that's something I've really been diving into for the last five years. On top of that everyone is encouraged to work in their Unique Ability, so I've become even more cognizant of the value I create. None of my previous positions challenged me to do much goal setting, so I also appreciate the way Coach helps me learn to set SMART goals for myself.

I've passed my two-year mark working with Shannon, and I can say I have never been bored—not even one day. Even when it slows for a bit, it comes as a welcome relief, and I know it won't last long. This position always has a ton of moving pieces, projects, and competing priorities, which provide the mental stimulation my previous roles lacked. Because Strategic Coach is continually growing and changing, I get to create new systems and adjust old ones, and I love that my contributions are continually increasing.

The other aspect of being an Executive Assistant that is tremendously attractive to me is the relationship we get to build. Anyone who knows me well knows that surface-level communication won't fulfill me. I am happiest when I can have deep conversations about life and the future. I love the fact that Strategic Coach is so relationship-focused and individuals are genuinely valued.

Working with Shannon allows me to have those deeper conversations. I love aligning with her on her goals and her future and then taking action to make sure they come to fruition. Yes, Shannon is technically my boss, but I feel like I am the leader in terms of making sure we stay focused on the goal, putting all the pieces together, and connecting with the team to make sure we're on schedule.

I'm often the first person Shannon tells things, and I don't take that lightly. Trust is such an important concept to me, so knowing Shannon trusts me to be the gatekeeper of sensitive information is important. I also need to feel like the person I'm supporting is worth supporting. So, I value Shannon's feedback. I respect her and the others I support on this team, and I want them to be successful.

I've never had so much input in my supportive roles! I enjoy my autonomy. No one dictates to me, and I'm never micromanaged. I get to take initiative instead of waiting for hierarchical approval. Shannon tells me her goals, gives me guidelines, and I make it happen.

This job comes so naturally to me, I seldom feel like I'm working against my grain, so most things feel easy. I love that I can just show up as myself and do work I love while still being challenged (in the best way!)

Katrina,

Thank You for all the amazing and deep support you gift me with! I was looking at the calendar this morning—with all the notes to go along with the meetings—and felt this deep sense of appreciation for what you do. You keep innovating new ways to make things work and flow, and it allows me to do what I do and not get bogged down doing things I suck at!

Your partnership helps me feel more confident about responding to people appropriately, and I'm no longer the bottleneck. You build in space when you know I need it, help me make good decisions about travel and what's realistic (although I know I push those boundaries), and maybe, most importantly, give me the confidence to say, "No."

Because of you, I've grown enormously. You kept me sane when I took on a whole new role while not giving up anything, and somehow, you found room for all the most important priorities so that everything and everyone got taken care of. Expert-level Tetris, indeed!

> *I love our deep conversations, how much you care about me, how much you trust me with what's important to you, and your ability to help me see things from others' points of view. We're good for each other. :)*
>
> *I LOVE our partnership. You are a gift in my life, my friend! I'm very, very grateful for you, Shannon*
>
> *And to Nicole – I would not be who I am or as good a partner without your expert coaching and guidance. We supported each other through all the things, and from you, I learned that I truly could have a Support Partner with whom I could trust everything that's important to me. You gently tugged the baton out of my hands, ensured that we handled any communication issues immediately so they didn't build up, and were always lovingly honest with me. You shared your incredible Strategic strengths with me and my clients to ensure that everything ran smoothly. You even created the Teamwork Tips guide so that other assistants could learn how to work with people like me. I'm so appreciative that as you transitioned to your next career that we remain, and always will be, dear friends.*
>
> *—So grateful for you,*
> *Shannon*

Leslie Loves Her Vital Backstage Role in Ryan's Life

College theater gave me my first taste of the importance of the backstage crew. Initially, I wanted one of the lead roles. However, I ended up choosing the role of technical director. That's when I recognized the significance of my role in the success of the play. And despite not being in the limelight, I truly loved it.

My initial administrative assistant job gave me an opportunity to do a mix of office work and fieldwork. I learned a great deal while working at the events company. However, while the experience provided fulfillment and exposure to veterans in the industry, the seven-days-a-week atmosphere left me exhausted.

For the next seven years, I moved up the ladder at a Japanese language company where the environment was significantly better. I found myself in various positions I hadn't initially realized I had the capabilities for. I took on the roles of administrative assistant, marketing specialist, and account manager and was involved in sales, accounting, and procurement. I felt driven to excel in every position, and I grew immensely, both professionally and personally. I eventually became the head of the administrative department as well as a corporate planning officer and finally, an Executive Assistant. These seven years helped me realize I enjoy providing support to the company. They also solidified my career aspiration to be an Executive Assistant.

Working in all those positions helped me see my potential and recognize my capability to continually do more. I also discovered how much I loved being able to support my community and watch the tasks I handled contribute to growth. Plus, I enjoyed the variety of the day-to-day with no set pattern.

Moving into the Executive Assistant position gave me a sense of independence I never had before. Though I work to support an entrepreneur, I have significant responsibilities and enjoy the freedom of decision-making. I feel like an extension of the entrepreneur, effectively becoming his second brain.

My favorite part of this job is being the support behind the curtain. The ability to contribute to the growth of Ryan and the company in critical ways is a passion close to my heart. I take growth seriously. In every situation, I ensure I always leave with a lesson. So, I appreciate the challenges and opportunities for growth this role brings. Each day varies, but it consistently offers valuable learning experiences.

To be honest, I wasn't even aware of my unique abilities until not long ago. I just knew that I loved what I was doing and enjoyed being part of the growth. But as I grew, I realized the importance of knowing myself at that level—that place where I can say with confidence, "I am capable of doing this, and this is where I excel." And now that I'm more aware of my Unique Abilities, my drive for growth fuels my need to continuously improve upon them.

I love that even though my job as Executive Assistant gets less prominence than managerial or other leadership roles, it is equally vital to the mission of the company. It reminds me of my theater role in college—behind the scenes but crucial to the overall success.

Dear Leslie,

I am so deeply appreciative of the partnership we have and the role you play in my life. You've been a vital part of my growth and Superpowers' growth. Your consistency, accountability, and thoughtfulness have been invaluable. I know I don't always make it easy, but you gracefully keep me organized and help me maintain a sense of calm every day.

Beyond work, your support has helped me maintain a balanced personal life. I know Carissa is especially grateful for that! From making sure I have time for lunch to helping plan date night, your efforts and thoughtfulness make it possible for me to remain present and in the moment.

> *To Amber, my first Executive Assistant and the person who kicked off this incredible journey, I am so deeply proud to witness your progress over the last decade. You personify what it means to achieve new levels of freedom and growth and are an inspiration to the entire team.*
>
> *With thanks,*
> *Ryan*

One of the Most Important Roles in the Company

As entrepreneurs and business leaders, we can't begin to show Celeena, Katrina, and Leslie how much we value the contributions they bring to our lives—not just in the professional setting, but also in the way they free us to be better parents, spouses, friends, and human beings in general. We hope we've demonstrated the fact that the role of Executive Assistant is anything but subordinate or subservient. Not one of us can imagine going back to the drudgery of our lives without our Executive Assistants.

If you still have questions about how you can find an EA or get training for you or your Executive Assistant (Yes, you probably need training on how to most effectively use an EA), keep reading. We've acquired quite a bit of knowledge getting to this place in our quest for freedom and growth, and we're willing to share.

Ryan's Biggest Takeaways from His EA Experience

Today, I work with a different EA, and though Amber set the bar high, Leslie brings at least as much skill and care to the table. Amber introduced me to the freedom and growth I could experience with an Executive Assistant. I was tremendously impressed with Amber's genuine compassion for me and my team. She has incredible ability paired with incredible care. One moment, she took it upon herself to do what she could to help every person in the office perform at their highest level. The next she ensured everyone's coffee was topped off and we were all fed. Amber sensed stress in the office and supported our team emotionally.

Amber also had an unceasing hunger for knowledge and gaining new capabilities. Because of her amazing push to grow and move forward, she changed roles when we started Superpowers, becoming an owner as well as our Chief Happiness Officer.

Leslie demonstrates this same passion for growth, but the thing I appreciate most is the way she demonstrates the same care and concern Amber brought to the role. Even an ocean away, Leslie has a genuine desire to help me succeed, which in turn ripples out to our entire team, the business, and even our clients.

You Can Be Superpowered

In any moment of decision,
the best thing you can do is the right thing,
the next best thing is the wrong thing,
and the worst thing you can do is nothing.

—Theodore Roosevelt

You're down to the last chapter, but we don't want you to finish reading until you've made a definitive decision to do something. Anything. We don't want this book to be a bit of information you tuck away for later. I wish you could see the excitement we feel when we watch people move from Superstressed to Superpowered. We are energized when you are transformed.

- Will you start the hiring process for an Executive Assistant this afternoon?
- Perhaps you'll begin habit-stacking to get the most out of the EA relationship you currently have.
- Will today be the day your mindset shifts, you see your true potential, jump off the seesaw, and discover you can have it all?
- Or, maybe you're like us. You've found your Superpower, and you read this book so you could pass it along to someone else who needs to be transformed.

Regardless of which one describes you—
today is the day to get started!

Go Ahead! Write Down Your Next Action Step

You Can Have it All

What if you could have

- The ability to do the work you're good at and have the life you want?
- More freedom to go after more high-impact work and projects that excite you?
- More time to spend with your family and explore new opportunities?
- Two new hours each week to enhance your unique abilities or just breathe?
- A bigger vision for the future and see more people transformed?
- Money to give away?

These are just a few things Superpowered business leaders see and feel every day. But to be truly Superpowered, your mindset must reach transformation level in every area of your business. This concept of developing relationships shouldn't be limited to your EA, it needs to flow over into your entire team. The most profitable businesses encourage everyone to do

> **There's no way any of us can be freed up to do our Unique Ability unless we're surrounded by people free to work in their unique abilities. –Shannon Waller**

what they love to do and do best because people working in their unique abilities will always run circles around people who are merely competent or good enough.

We also noticed that nearly every entrepreneur experiencing both freedom and growth has an Executive Assistant clearing the roadblocks. It's not that their businesses don't face obstacles and challenges. These key leaders have all the pain points that prevent other entrepreneurs and teams from doing their best and highest work. However, they've uncovered the secret. They understand the vital nature of their Executive Assistant.

The three of us work passionately to help entrepreneurs achieve new levels of freedom and growth. We want to enable entrepreneurs to achieve their vision, realize their dreams, maximize their potential, and grow the people around them. And we believe if you get the Executive Assistant position filled correctly, build a relationship, and offer the right training, coaching, and ongoing growth opportunities, you can move your business and your life from mediocre or barely surviving to amazingly superpowered.

When you're exhausted, you become reactive. A task becomes a problem, and every problem becomes a crisis. New creative thoughts don't come. And even if they do, you find yourself shelving them one after another. For the entrepreneur who thrives on brainstorming and moving forward with the next exciting plan, life without an Executive Assistant can become soul-crushing. He or she needs time for rejuvenation; however, they feel like the sun won't rise in the east if they don't do it themselves. Though they think they're in control, it's really stress running the show.

Moving From SUPERSTRESSED		Moving To SUPERPOWERED
Menial	→	Meaningful
Micro-Managing	→	Being Managed
Short-Term Mindset	→	Long-Term Mindset
Settling For Freedom Or Growth	→	Achieving Freedom And Growth
Task-Oriented	→	Team-Oriented
Suck	→	Success
Production At -10x	→	10x Impact And Production
Frustration	→	Fun

When you find your way to the Superpowered side of the scale, you'll discover all those menial tasks become meaningful to your EA. The drain of micro-managing will transform into a relief of being managed. A short-term mindset shoots into the long-term, and you no longer pick and choose between freedom or growth; you have it all!

At Strategic Coach and Superpowers, we want task-oriented businesses to become team-oriented enterprises because that will turn the Suck into Success and take your production from negative to immensely more than you can imagine.

And best of all, when you move from anywhere on the scale to Superpowered, your Frustration turns into Fun!

It took me forever to figure it out; however, I've discovered when I start feeling captured, squished, or small, that's my clue that I'm not utilizing my support system.
–Shannon Waller

When we limit ourselves to only what we can do and control, our futures shrink. We limit ourselves because we can't think any bigger. We don't have the time or capacity to see an expanded future. Not only is there a ceiling, but it seems to be lowering the longer we strive.

However, when we have the right kind of support, our futures become immeasurable. Surrounded by Unique Ability teamwork, the vision of what's possible expands exponentially. Executive Assistants remove the ceiling on what we can do personally as well as for our teams.

Strategic Coach Wants to Superpower Your Thinking

At Strategic Coach, we help entrepreneurs think about their thinking. We want to help entrepreneurs grow their businesses by expanding their minds and changing the way they think about their role within their businesses. Dan Sullivan boils it down to, "Always make your future bigger than your past."

You'll need Strategic Coach's 4 C's formula as you step into this adventure of making your future bigger. Everything you've read in this book begins with commitment. You must commit to believing in yourself, Supershifting your mindset, and adding a personal manager to your team.

> Strategic Coach has helped me optimize my life and business in ways I could've never imagined. The thinking tools, the community, and the coaches have all enriched my life beyond words.
> —Kary Oberbrunner, Founder and CEO of Igniting Souls

Strategic Coach calls this person a Strategic Assistant, and we begin talking about the importance of this Who in one of the entrepreneur's first sessions. We also offer training for the Strategic Assistants that helps them understand the transformation their entrepreneurs will undergo as they work within the Coach community.

We're extremely excited that Superpowers, as clients of Strategic Coach, utilizes so many of the Strategic Coach concepts in how they run their business. We believe their philosophy and the 10X thinking entrepreneurs develop in their Coach session pair together well.

Ryan's First Executive Assistant

After I attended my initial Strategic Coach meeting, I set out to find the perfect "Who" to complement my "How." And one of the first things I did after hiring Amber was sign her up for Coach's Strategic Assistant program. Their training actually outpaces the entrepreneurial sessions, so she quickly moved ahead of me in terms of what I would learn through Coach. I believe this added training catapulted my success in Strategic Coach as well as building my business.

Superpowers Process

At Superpowers, we love working with Strategic Coach clients. After working with their personal coach and the Strategic Coach team, these individuals think about things differently than the average entrepreneur. And, as we've said, the SuperShifted

Strategic Coach is the single best investment I've made in my life.
−Steven Neuner

Mindset takes you from Superstressed to Superpowered in the shortest period of time.

Helping successful entrepreneurs achieve new levels of freedom and growth drives us at Superpowers. So, before we go out and look for the perfect Who to manage you, we meet with you for an in-depth interview. We focus on your Unique Ability and explore the things that get in the way of you being immersed in it every minute that you're at work.

Superpowers also offers the 3Cs of Curriculum, Coaching, and Community for Executive Assistants. Even companies that have not used Superpowers EA placement services can benefit from the 3Cs. From bi-weekly coaching calls to the playbook library and our community of EAs, you set your Executive Assistant up for success when you get in on the Superpowers membership-based program.

You won't find many placement services that also train the entrepreneur; however, Superpowers has found that having an outside person focused on identifying the solutions that work best for a business leader's specific situation proves invaluable. Members have access to our Chief Happiness Officer, who acts as a sounding board, coach, and accountability partner. We've found that the extra training and support supercharges the EA-Entrepreneur relationship and puts it on the fast track to exponential growth.

> **SuperPowers gave us the gift of time to think big and execute our vision, all thanks to the unparalleled support from our strategic assistant, Joy.**
> **–Dan Fraser, NextKey Services**

Ryan Beagin came to Superpowers because he couldn't keep up with his Quickbooks and his rapidly growing company, and like many, he was skeptical:

> *When I initially went through the evaluation process with Superpowers, I had serious doubts they would be able to find someone who met my "perfect candidate" criteria. Self-motivated, independent, patient, flexible, and intuitive were at the top of my list. Clarisse has not only been all these things, but you could add innovative, thoughtful, creative, intelligent, eager, and, most notably, HAPPY! We are all waiting for her to have her first bad day. —Ryan Beagin, Tabs Payment Solutions*

One of the evaluation tools Superpowers uses is the Strategic Coach Experience Transformer®. This process provides an endless feedback loop that gives our business leaders and Executive Assistants an opportunity to see what's working and what needs improvement. Putting this simple strategy into play can be the difference between a six-month sprint with your EA and a six-year relationship. The basic principle lies in asking three questions of every big event. Regardless of the outcome—good or bad—when you ask these three questions, you increase your ability to work faster, easier, cheaper, and bigger in the future:

1. What worked?
2. What didn't work?
3. If I could do this over, how would I do it better? Or how can I replicate that?

By evaluating each situation in this light, we gain wisdom and eliminate blame and excuses. Nothing matters except learning, growth, and progress.

Ryan Talks about the Beginning of Superpowers

Steven and I both built our first businesses the hard way. We felt like we spent those years feeling around in the dark. So, when we started talking about creating Superpowers, we were adamantly determined to apply everything we had learned in Strategic Coach. I combined everything I learned from my first endeavor to bake a vision for Superpowers as well as a real estate investment platform I own.

It's Time

Strategic Coach and Superpowers have a common mission. We both want to empower entrepreneurs. It hurts our souls to see burned out, depressed, superstressed women and men striving outside their unique abilities with little to show for all their hard work. We believe in the message of Dan Sullivan and Benjamin Hardy's book *10x Is Easier Than 2x™*, and we want to help business leaders discover the freedom and growth that comes with 10X impact. Our passion is to be a hero to these brave individuals who risk it all to live their dreams.

> **Maximizer is one of my Unique Ability traits. I am fueled when I can help someone be freed up to maximize their capabilities.**
> **–Shannon Waller**

So, if you're living in the land of Delegation, Frustration, Resignation, or Depression, it's time to move. Commit to yourself and your business today. Schedule a Discovery call at StrategicCoach.com or SuperpowersHQ.com and let us help you become turbo-charged and Superpowered.

Resources

The following free resources are available at
SuperpoweredBook.com

- The Ideal Assistant Blueprint will help you fill out the "My Perfect Day" section.
- 12 Stages of Burnout Guide
- The Entrepreneurial Attitude exercise
- Strategic Coach Impact Filter
- The full list of questions Superpowers asks at the end of the first three months
- The Communication Builder
- The Entrepreneurial Time System
- Teamwork Tips Handout

Endnotes

1   Bailey, Danielle Alexander. *LinkedIn*. "The Five Most Famous Assistants (You Never Knew Existed). August 16, 2023. https://www.linkedin.com/pulse/5-most-famo us-assistants-you-never-knew-existed-alexander-bailey

2   *Pew Research Center*. "Modern Parenthood." March 14, 2023. https://www.pewresearch.org/social-trends/2013/ 03/14/modern-parenthood-roles-of-moms-and-dads- converge-as-they-balance-work-and-family/

3   Integrator is a title we adopted from the Entrepreneurial Operating System (EOS).

4   Kleiner, Kurt. *Scientific American*. "Lunchtime Leniency: Judges' Rulings Are Harsher When They Are Hungrier." September 2011. https://www. scientificamerican.com/article/lunchtime-leniency/.

5   Cassin, Ryan. *Superpowers HQ*. "Entrepreneur Mental Health Statistics." Accessed May 23, 2024. https:// superpowershq.com/entrepreneur-mental-health-statistics/

About the Authors

Shannon Waller

Shannon Waller, seasoned expert on entrepreneurs and entrepreneurial teams, has been with Strategic Coach® since 1991. She is renowned for creating The Strategic Coach Team® Programs, including the Strategic Assistant™ Program, designed to cultivate a winning Entrepreneurial Attitude among team members.

As a key collaborator, speaker, and author, Shannon's work emphasizes conative excellence and provides actionable strategies for team success. She shares these principles in her books The Team Success Handbook and Multiplication By Subtraction and as co-author of the bestselling book Unique Ability® 2.0: Discovery.

Ryan Cassin

Ryan Cassin is passionate about entrepreneurship, having started and sold multiple businesses over the last decade. In 2020, he co-founded Superpowers, which helps entrepreneurs achieve new levels of freedom and growth by hiring and training their right-fit Executive Assistant.

Cassin is also a co-founder of Here Homes, a single-family real estate rental platform with homes in markets throughout the Southeast.

Cassin is a former president of Entrepreneurs' Organization Dallas and serves on the Entrepreneurs' Organization Global Governance Committee.

He currently resides in Dallas, Texas, with his wife, Carissa.

Steven Neuner

A lifetime entrepreneur and learner, Steven Neuner has built, scaled, and exited multi-million-dollar companies without sacrificing his life priorities by building championship teams. As a coach and mentor to successful entrepreneurs, Steven's passion is helping them reach new levels of freedom and growth.

On Free Days, you might find Steven on a date with his best friend, wife, and business partner, Corey, at BarnHill Vineyards, their boutique vineyard and live music venue. They also enjoy embarking on family adventures with their three children, huge extended family, and closest friends. For more, please visit StevenJNeuner.com.

BUSINESS COACHING FOR
GROWTH-MINDED ENTREPRENEURS

Strategic Coach® is an organization run by entrepreneurs for entrepreneurs. We've worked with more than 20,000 successful business owners from around the globe to help them achieve faster growth, greater profits, and an exceptional quality of life.

For additional resources, scan the QR code:

Or go to strategiccoach.com/go/superpowered

superpowers

Superpowers helps successful entrepreneurs achieve new levels of freedom and growth. Our executive assistants anticipate your unique needs so you stay focused on your highest-leverage activities.

superpowershq.com

superpowers

Bonus Bundle

Scan the QR code to learn more

THIS BOOK IS PROTECTED INTELLECTUAL PROPERTY

Instant IP™

The author of this book values Intellectual Property. The book you just read is protected by Instant IP™, a proprietary process, which integrates blockchain technology giving Intellectual Property "Global Protection." By creating a "Time-Stamped" smart contract that can never be tampered with or changed, we establish "First Use" that tracks back to the author.

Instant IP™ functions much like a Pre-Patent™ since it provides an immutable "First Use" of the Intellectual Property. This is achieved through our proprietary process of leveraging blockchain technology and smart contracts. As a result, proving "First Use" is simple through a global and verifiable smart contract. By protecting intellectual property with blockchain technology and smart contracts, we establish a "First to File" event.

Protected by Instant IP™

LEARN MORE AT INSTANTIP.TODAY

Printed in the USA
CPSIA information can be obtained
at www.ICGtesting.com
JSHW011205111124
73358JS00004B/6